Banking in Turmoil

Also by Steven I. Davis

AFTER THE CREDIT CRISIS: Best Practice in Banking the High Net Worth Individual

BANCASSURANCE: The Lessons of Global Experience in Banking and Insurance Collaboration

BANK MERGERS AND ACQUISITIONS: The Lessons of Global Experience

BANK MERGERS: Lessons for the Future

BEST PRACTICE IN BANKING THE AFFLUENT

CROSS-SELLING IN RETAIL BANKING: Meeting the Revenue Growth Challenge

EXCELLENCE IN BANKING

INVESTMENT BANKING: Addressing the Management Issues

LEADERSHIP IN CONFLICT: The Lessons of History

LEADERSHIP IN FINANCIAL SERVICES

MANAGING CHANGE IN THE EXCELLENT BANKS

THE MANAGEMENT FUNCTION IN INTERNATIONAL BANKING

THE EURO-BANK

Banking in Turmoil

Strategies for Sustainable Growth

Steven I. Davis

Managing Director, Davis International Banking Consultants

First published 2009 by
PALGRAVE MACMILLAN

Palgrave Macmillan in the UK is an imprint of Macmillan Publishers Limited,
registered in England, company number 785998, of Houndmills, Basingstoke,
Hampshire RG21 6XS.

Palgrave Macmillan in the US is a division of St Martin's Press LLC,
175 Fifth Avenue, New York, NY 10010.

Palgrave Macmillan is the global academic imprint of the above companies
and has companies and representatives throughout the world.

Palgrave® and Macmillan® are registered trademarks in the United States,
the United Kingdom, Europe and other countries.

ISBN-13: 978–0–230–23571–7 hardback

This book is printed on paper suitable for recycling and made from fully
managed and sustained forest sources. Logging, pulping and manufacturing
processes are expected to conform to the environmental regulations of the
country of origin.

A catalogue record for this book is available from the British Library.

A catalog record for this book is available from the Library of Congress.

10   9   8   7   6   5   4   3   2   1
18   17   16   15   14   13   12   11   10   09

Printed and bound in Great Britain by
CPI Antony Rowe, Chippenham and Eastbourne

Contents

List of Figures

List of Interviews

1
Introduction

The global banking world has been transformed by the crisis which commenced in mid-2007 and reached a climax – for the time being! – in October 2008 with a firestorm which brought about the collapse of a number of US and other banking institutions and an entry of government ownership and intervention unprecedented since the 1930s.

The overall objective of this book is to provide insights into what bankers, their regulators, investors, advisors and other constituencies have learned from this traumatic experience with a view to planning for the future. It draws on a series of 25 in-depth interviews with such senior executives as well as the research carried out by official bodies such as the International Monetary Fund, consulting firms and bank analysts.

Written in early 2009, it cannot pretend to draw a line under a crisis whose evolution has consistently confounded the so-called experts. This show will run and run! But bank management must manage for the future on the basis of the evidence available. Some business models are destined for the junk heap, while others may evolve in a different direction. Bank regulators, governments and rating agencies must shape their policies to reflect the new realities. And perhaps most interesting of all, bank investors must review their former growth model for bank stocks, which arguably has been a major driver of the banking crisis.

More specifically, as strategy consultants our focus in this volume will be on strategic models which should stand the test of time in this new banking world. To anchor this analysis in the real world, we profile a number of actual case studies of successful major banking institutions across the world. Each is based on a business model which, in the view of our interviewees, has navigated the crisis to date with success and is likely to continue to do so.

In making this selection, we acknowledge that the current crisis has scarred virtually every possible candidate for inclusion in the list, and experience since 2007 has clearly demonstrated the limitations of projecting past results! Yet we believe that the generic lessons are valid and offer at least the basis on which other banks might ground their own strategy.

We commence the body of this analysis with Chapter 2, which briefly summarizes how the crisis evolved from July 2007 until the end of 2008 with its transformation of banking structures and ownership. Our focus is on the contributing factors, the data which track its evolution and the new insights obtained as the crisis evolves. Avid readers of the financial press, in particular the *Financial Times*, may wish to skip over this chapter, but for others it may be a useful explanation of how losses on a segment of the US mortgage market morphed into the worst global banking and economic crisis since the US meltdown in the 1930s.

The insights from our interview series and data analysis commence with Chapter 3, which provides the answers to a central question with which we opened each interview: 'what have we learned from this experience which is relevant for future planning?' Our interview base includes senior bankers (including two chairmen of major global banks), regulators in the US and UK, the major rating agencies, and experienced bank analysts and management consultants from leading firms in major financial centres.

The dominant issue in the 'turmoil' has been risk management, and Chapter 4 addresses the lessons of experience since mid-2007. In sum, how might the various constituencies – the banks themselves, investors, rating agencies, governments and regulators – improve their ability to detect and resolve issues which by the end of 2008 have generated over a trillion dollars of losses for the banks alone, quite apart from other financial institutions and investors? While many of these constituencies have yet to agree a new regulatory framework, its possible outlines are beginning to take shape.

Chapter 5 focuses on business models – in effect, the strategic decisions made to allocate resources – as well as perennial issues, such as that of size and complexity, which now raise new questions in a quasi-nationalized banking world. The three core strategic dimensions – client base, product line and geographic scope – are each addressed on the basis of our interview series.

The related issues of leadership and culture are the focus of Chapter 6. In our earlier books on best practice in bank management, we have found that these 'soft' issues are central to bank performance, and the recent turnover of top management in troubled banks has given added meaning to the issue of the ability of senior bankers to manage a large and complex business.

Chapter 7 provides the views of industry analysts and our interviewees on the likely evolution of banking profits and returns on equity over the intermediate term. A number of useful empirical studies, usually based on data from previous banking and economic cycles going back to the 1930s, provide a useful consensus on the intermediate term outlook for bank profits and returns on investment in the new environment. Such views are understandably couched in tentative terms, given the uncertainties in particular for the real world economic impact of the banking crisis in 2009–2010, but also for the issue of valuing the toxic exposures many banks continue to carry on their balance sheets.

Our focus on bank strategies continues with Chapter 8, which profiles a number of banking institutions cited by our interviewees as successful business models which might be relevant for their peers. As indicated above, such past success is no guarantee of future results, but the models may be useful to peer banks and other constituencies. Every effort has been made to select cases from a variety of banks from different sectors and geographies. The format of the case studies includes a brief profile of the bank, analysis of its basic strategy and our views on the possible outlook for the future.

Chapter 9 provides a brief summary of our findings as well as our interviewees' and our own view of the outlook for the future for banking strategies. A particular effort has been made to identify issues which have not been resolved by this crisis and may reasonably be expected to recur in the future, and those policies and mechanisms which hopefully will be put in place to prevent such a repeat performance.

2
From Sub-Prime to Quasi-Nationalization: The Unique Elements of a Banking Crisis

The International Monetary Fund (IMF) in its research has identified over 100 banking cycles in recent history, but the current turmoil is unique in its scope, magnitude, and likely impact on the real economy. This chapter will focus on data and graphics, rather than text, to highlight the key dimensions of the turmoil. The textual dimension has been – and will continue to be! – the subject of thousands of penetrating articles and books, and one picture is truly worth a thousand words! We also focus on the features which have made it unique in some 70 years of banking history.

To summarize briefly, at the outset, the 2007–2009 crisis – and its likely economic impact – has been characterized to date by the following key global drivers:

- *An extended period of economic boom,* following the dotcom collapse in 2001–2002, which encouraged risk-taking across the banking system. The boom in many markets like the US took the form of house price inflation which lifted housing loans in particular to unprecedented multiples of GDP.
- *Macro-economic imbalances* in the form of massive trade surpluses in key emerging markets as well as a global explosion in financial assets. The result was a so-called wall of money seeking yield and growth in the financial markets, which drove risk premia to historically low levels.
- *Increased leverage* not only in the US and other banking systems but also in non-bank institutions – the so-called shadow banking

system which largely escaped regulatory control. Such institutions as off-balance sheet special investment vehicles (SIVs), finance companies, insurers and hedge funds in turn relied for enhanced yield on maturity mismatch by short date funding, which melted away in the subsequent de-leveraging period.

- *Complex financial instruments*, usually based on derivative products and often on mortgage assets, which met the demand for enhanced yield. Prime ratings were offered by the rating agencies to create an apparent yield premium over comparable traditional rated securities. Today billions of dollars of such outstanding 'toxic' assets as collateralized debt obligations (CDOs) on bank balance sheets cannot realistically be valued to provide the basis for their sale as occurred in the US in the 1980s' savings bank crisis.

- *The introduction* (after many years of debate) *of mark-to-market accounting* for risk assets, which has obliged many financial institutions to write down not only market-quoted assets but also those for which no market price existed but were clearly worth less than their book value. In previous banking crises such as the Latin American losses in the 1980s, in contrast, all banks continued to carry such loans at par.

- *A massive wave of de-leveraging across the world* by institutions and individual investors who sold what could be sold and what was perceived vulnerable to such de-leveraging. This vicious circle in October 2008 caused the collapse of many bank stocks and forced government-supported mergers in the US, UK and other markets.

The history of this banking crisis is best told in graphic form. A series of such graphs prepared by consultants McKinsey & Co track the evolution of sub-prime housing loans made in the US into complex derivative-based instruments, which ignited the combustible material from structural imbalances in global monetary flows and the advent of aggressive new asset builders such as hedge funds, private equity firms and sovereign risk funds. Sub-prime mortgage loans are those which did not meet traditional credit criteria such as loan-to-value ratios and proof of income.

Thus Figure 2.1 profiles the speculative bubble created by these forces in the period leading up to the crisis in 2007.

Figure 2.2 shows how sub-prime mortgage loans created the raw material for structured products whose risk was ultimately absorbed

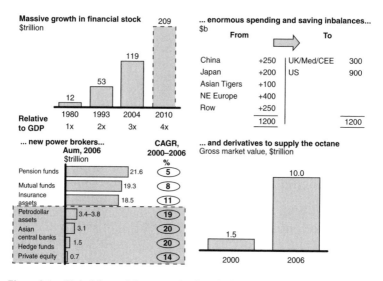

Figure 2.1 Global financial system: built to bubble

Source: McKinsey & Co – International Bank Planners Forum Presentation, November 2007.

not only by banks but also by pension funds, hedge funds and money market funds. Unlike the traditional home mortgage loan made by a bank that presumably is well able to evaluate the borrower's credit, many of these loans were actually created without the intervention of such a bank but rather by brokers and other intermediaries, who each added their margin to the finished product.

The process of creating a CDO from such sub-prime loans and derivatives is summarized in Figure 2.3. It also tracks its composition from 2002 to 2006, when residential mortgage-backed securities (RMBS) based on sub-prime credit default swaps virtually replaced all other assets comprising the CDO. Clearly, sub-prime mortgage assets were in abundant supply as such raw material to meet the surging demand for assets providing a premium yield and acceptable rating.

The final step in this process was to leverage the resulting mortgage-backed security. A number of tranches of varying degrees of seniority thus enhanced the original yield on the sub-prime asset, which represented the equity core of the product with only some 3% of the total package. Perhaps the bulk – from 30–100% – of this leverage took the form of so-called super-senior paper which received

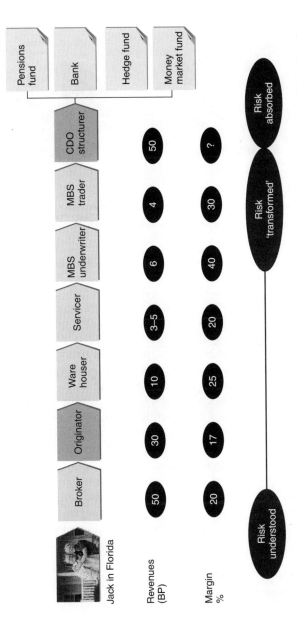

Figure 2.2 The particular incentives and opacity of the US sub-prime made it the 'San Andreas fault' of global banking
Source: McKinsey & Co – International Bank Planners Forum Presentation, November 2007.

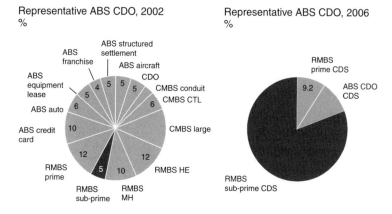

Representative ABS CDO, 2002
%

Representative ABS CDO, 2006
%

Note. ABS – asset-backed securities; CDO – collateralized debt obligation, CMBS – commercial mortgage-backed securities; CTL – credit tenant lease; HE – home equity; MH – manufactured housing; RMBS – residential mortgage-backed securities; CDS – credit default swap.

Figure 2.3   CDOs became highly concentrated...
Source: McKinsey & Co – International Bank Planners Forum Presentation, November 2007.

a prime AAA rating from the agencies. When the equity tranche, made up of the CDO itself, went into default, one by one the more senior tranches were endangered (Figure 2.4).

Thus domestic mortgage loans in the US were structured, leveraged and marketed to investors across the world, usually by intermediaries such as investment banks which had created them.

This product of the bubble in the US market, however, interacted with two other variables to create, in effect, three different crises. Figure 2.5 below, taken from a Boston Consulting Group (BCG) presentation, profiles the leverage and liquidity crises which have run in parallel with the asset quality issue.

Thus asset devaluation has combined with the de-leveraging process (needed to lower capital ratios) and the maturity mismatch of short funding (which has created a liquidity squeeze). Figure 2.6 profiles the resulting downward spiral which continues into 2009. Bank earnings reports for 2008 thus have reflected the steady attrition of the mark-to-market values of problem assets as the wave of de-leveraging sales erodes their perceived value, rather than the addition of new risks.

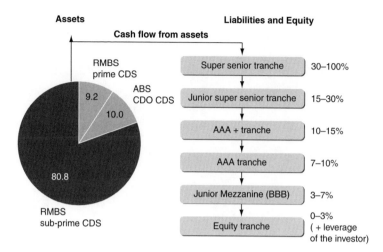

Figure 2.4 ... and highly leveraged
Source: McKinsey & Co – International Bank Planners Forum Presentation, November 2007.

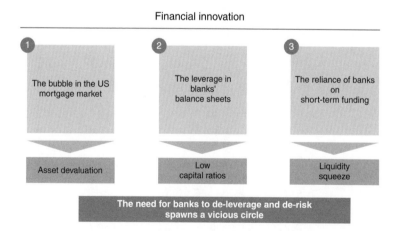

Figure 2.5 In a nutshell – there is not one crisis but three
Source: The Boston Consulting Group – International Bank Planners Forum Presentation, November 2008.

10

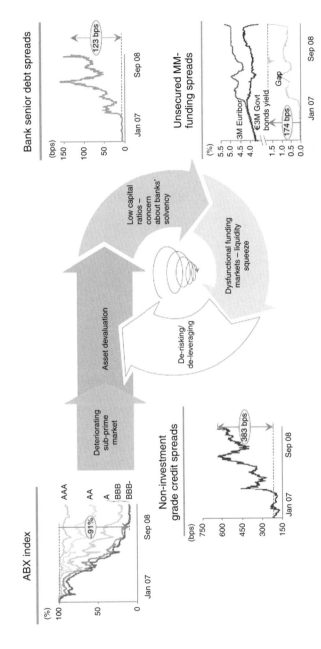

Figure 2.6 This created a vicious circle that sent the broader financial market into a downward spiral
Source: The Boston Consulting Group – International Bank Planners Forum Presentation, November 2008.

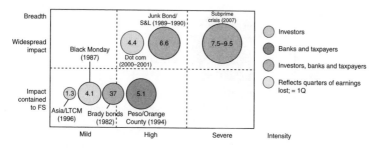

Figure 2.7   This is an unprecedented crisis...
Source: The Boston Consulting Group – International Bank Planners Forum Presentation, November 2008.

The final stage of the turmoil has been the impact of the banking crisis on economic activity – known as the 'real economy'. Whereas earlier banking problems had little or no significant effect on economic activity, the current one has had a widespread negative impact on economies across the globe. Figure 2.7 from BCG thus ranks the current problem as the most severe in recent history, as the shrinkage of bank lending has devastated both developed and emerging economies.

The extent of the current crisis reflects both the skills of institutions that 'originated to distribute' such paper as well as the universality of demand for such investments. As indicated by Figure 2.8, banks were rivalled by money market funds as buyers of AAA asset-backed securities, followed by specialist credit funds, hedge funds, SIVs and conduits.

To quote one industry observer,

everybody joined the party!

No financial service models have been unscathed, although investment banks in particular have suffered. At the other extreme are the 'innocent bystanders' from Australia to Hong Kong to Norway – investors and institutions who were simply in search of a relatively attractive yield. The IMF in late 2008 estimated that total losses from the banking crisis to date totalled $1.4 trillion, of which

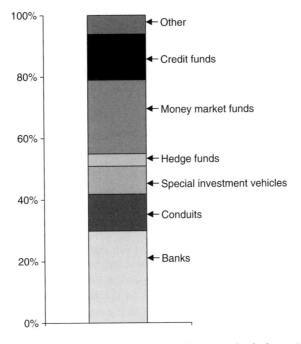

Figure 2.8   Components of a crisis – buyers of AAA asset-backed securities (%)
Source: Citigroup, Financial Times, DIBC analysis.

only $600 billion had by then been suffered by banks. In the US, the brokerage firm Sandler O'Neill estimates that losses from FDIC-insured banks to the end 2008 total $900 billion, which represented 67% of their current capital base.

3
Generic Lessons from the Turmoil: What Can We Do Better in the Future?

Our interview process began with the simple catch-all question: what have you learned from the crisis so you can do a better job in the future? The following chapters on risk management and other topics delve more deeply into specific issues, but it is interesting to explore what is top of mind of senior bankers and banking experts as they sort out the lessons of 2007–2009. In addition to summarizing the conclusions of our interviewees on the generic lessons from the turmoil, this chapter provides their detailed comments on the role of the much criticized rating agencies. Chapter 5 on future business models incorporates such reflections on the investor model and role of regulators, two key drivers of these models.

Overall lessons from the banking crisis

Perhaps the most frequent and powerful response relates to the need for relevant (especially risk management) experience and wisdom at the top of the bank. In a word, top management must take responsibility for their banks' poor performance during the crisis.

A veteran of the banking wars is Sir Win Bischoff, the former chairman of Citigroup, whose long and distinguished career in banking had traversed many banking trauma before he was named Chairman during the crisis:

> If you look back at history, there's a commonality to practically all the major banking crises: leverage and real estate! Gut feel and experience may or may not be essential, but this time the lessons

of history didn't sink in. When you're making lots of money it may be too good to last. I don't believe the risk processes were wrong, but the judgements based on them were. Looking at the performance of the major banks recently, the relatively more successful ones were those who had several people at the top who had risk management experience and lots of gut feel; that arguably is better than technological competence.

His views are echoed by Tom Hill, head of the strategy team at UBS, another bank that suffered heavily from the turmoil:

> Make an analogy with steering a ship – perhaps the Titanic. Even if you rely on systems to avoid an iceberg, you should also use what the navies in the US and UK call a Mark 1 eyeball – an actual person who is the lookout, even if you have wonderful systems. UBS built sophisticated risk control systems, but they were too complicated and powerful for anyone in the bank to second guess. Is that people or process? Ultimately, people.

A cry of despair comes from another banking veteran, Robert Albertson, head of strategy of investment bank Sandler O'Neill in New York:

> Each banking crisis is the same old stuff. The issues aren't solved. This one is more severe. The risk managers don't look at the forest, just the trees. They don't see the whole picture until too late! Blaming bad underwriting, flawed products and securitization, for example, misses the point. No one recognised the impact of the massive liquidity in the system from emerging market surpluses; it came upon us out of nowhere! Two years ago mortgage lenders examined the market in minute detail for each loan vintage, found no negative amortization and concluded 'this is great'! But look at their assumptions for stress: they all assuming house prices would *increase* – at rates from 5 to 20% per annum. Not even a zero rate! So it had nothing to do with the product, but the banks' assumptions.

> Everyone on the planet ignored the forest! You can have all the information and good models, but garbage in is still garbage out.

No one took into consideration the emerging market surplus, and the regulators don't understand emerging markets!

Stephen Green, chairman of HSBC and during his career former head of the bank's treasury function, sums up the lessons he draws from the turmoil and the importance of management judgement:

> Mathematics will only take you so far – beyond that you need to understand the risk profile of the product. If things are too good to be true, they probably are! If the distributor and product provider don't understand the product, they have failed in their role. The combination of high/increasing leverage and greater product complexity has led to the meltdown.

Another guilty party is investor greed. The pre-crisis investor 'model' called for double digit annual earnings growth almost regardless of national market, and bank management in some mature markets struggled to meet that target.

Veteran European bank analyst Simon Samuels of Citigroup summarizes his conclusions:

> One major issue is demanding shareholders. Stockholders of banks in mature markets demanded compound annual growth rates of 10–15%; it's the story of the last decade. It's not by chance that hanks in Spain and Ireland didn't have much exposure to the shadow banking system because of good natural growth. Emerging markets may be higher risk but they didn't have to resort to higher leverage. The conclusion: equity investors have to lower their growth expectations.

This view is echoed from the bank's perspective, as confirmed by the CFO (chief financial officer) of a major European bank's asset management business:

> Risk models aren't the problem; they only throw off numbers. All the top management of banks want is growth! In banking, there hasn't been real risk management since 2001 at the top of banks.

Top management also comes in for criticism.

Roberto Nicastro of UniCredit acknowledges that

We need to listen less to the market when they purely ask for short term performance; it's better to look beyond the short and medium term. Short term pressures may push banks to be overambitious in business mix, organizational structure and risk taking. No bank can say now that 'we didn't listen then'. Everybody now has regrets: paying too much for, and doing too many, deals. It was market pressure.

Several of our interviewees emphasized the systemic failure which led to the crisis, with all players in the drama contributing to it.

Thus Andy Maguire of BCG expresses a philosophical view:

We're all part of the conspiracy of silence. Even with grey hairs, organisations still got into trouble. Go back to basics? But the next crisis won't be the same as the last one. It's always different. There are lessons from risk management: the tyranny of models. But people who used judgment also had troubles. There's no sense to it! It's a cultural thing, which makes it hard for regulators, since you can't measure it. You can look for the telltale signs. For example, everybody knew you shouldn't assume normal (Gaussian) distribution, but people still did.

Another veteran of the global banking scene, Robin Monro-Davies, former head of Fitch Ratings, agrees:

There are lots of people looking for the silver bullet; if we knew what it was, the crisis wouldn't have happened! What we had was a major bubble, and now we're looking for someone to blame. But it's everybody! Everyone had to be part of the consensus. To have stepped in at any time would have been very difficult. Can you see someone saying (during the boom) 'only 75% loan to value ratio (for home loans)? Are you mad? House prices will continue to rise!'

A senior US bank regulator makes the useful distinction between systemic and individual risks:

In hindsight, supervisors and regulators should have done a better job understanding and applying the supervision of systemic and individual firm risks. Systemic risks were not well captured in the supervision framework, especially as they were applied to individual institutions. We tended to look at the individual bank. For example, securitization activity seemed to allow firms to remove risky assets from the balance sheet, which was fine at the firm level. But, not much work was done in analyzing the systemic risks if everyone did it. Similarly, from a systemic view, we've learned that liquidity is not the same as firm-specific capital; it is a state of mind.

Fellow regulator Tom Huertas of the UK Financial Services Authority takes a similar philosophical stance:

The game can change: what we assume now might not last forever. All the old predictions were too good to last – and they didn't! We were victims of our own success. In the macro economy, the 'great moderation' created a mindset. After previous crises like the dotcom one, the markets roared back to even higher levels.

A final word on the lessons of the turmoil comes from a veteran investment banker:

What have we learned? First, every boom comes apart at the end. The whole banking system is pro-cyclical. All the players have to take responsibility; we are all the culprits. Second, there are so many multiple risks in play – globality, securitisation, etc. – and decisions on all these are usually being taken without a risk manager at the top of the origination. The banks have committed themselves to risk taking, but the individuals who run them, using questionable models like VaR, have to deal with complexities far beyond their grasp, and delegate decisions to technical people. How can you fix it? Can you combine all these different businesses? My big fear is that the pendulum will swing to the other side, with regulators putting constraints on management with the result that you have more, not better regulation.

The role of the rating agencies

In this context, our interviewees had few words of praise for the rating agencies, who are accused of conflicts of interest in their profitable role of supplying investment grade ratings for structured products, slowness in downgrading problem banks and defective models.

One London-based bank analyst summarizes a common view:

Agencies have to regain credibility; they're completely discredited. They need to demonstrate their independence or be broken up.

A New York banking consultant agrees:

The agencies' credibility is broken. There will be significant oversight and change. I'm amazed that they're still in business! There's a bowling ball coming down the alley!

Simon Samuels echoes this view:

The entire business model of the rating agencies has been broken. There's an inherent conflict of interest. The whole model has to change through government intervention or a new pricing model. They gave a health warning on CDOs to the effect that a CDO AAA is different from that of a corporate issuer – but the subtlety was lost and investors assumed they were the same.

Charles Wendel, a US banking consultant, adds:

They're a lagging indicator; the downgrades came only after the headlines in the newspapers. The people who got hurt were the mass investors. Everyone knows there was a conflict of interest.

A former senior rating agency executive acknowledges the problem:

Rating agencies are at the centre of the banking crisis. What can be done about it? The first step is to move away from excessive reliance on rating agencies. Banks made good money from a quick fix – a presumably risk-free AAA rated product: it's paradise!

AAA is the supreme prize: 'I have a risk free asset'. The hoax was perpetuated.

Banks have to remove themselves from this reliance. It can be done in two steps. First, regulators need to move away from the reliance on ratings under Basel II; it's a bad example to the market that implies they should rely on ratings. Second, the buy side has to do its own credit analysis. You can't say 'I don't understand it, but it's AAA'.

Eileen Fahey of Fitch Ratings in the US accepts the need for improvement:

Both banks and rating agencies need more stress testing on elements not seen in historic data. There should be more study of unexpected consequences which may have been ignored in the past and which could blow up a company. For ratings, there's too much reliance on what happened historically.

Our models will be reviewed, especially for sectors such as mortgage lending. We'll step back and ask what this data is actually telling us – what really differentiates an AAA credit from lesser ones, etc. Particular attention will be paid to CDO risk – with a more conservative posture and lower rating.

Another career senior bank rating executive in London adds:

We'll rotate people internally – moving them from fundamental analysis to the structured finance side. And we'll write reports on the specific assumptions in our models. There was an over-reliance on models; you need to use gut instinct as an override on the models.

Other observers provide more broadly based suggestions for the future.

A senior US regulator makes some thoughtful comments:

We don't yet know the lessons (for rating agencies in the future); we're still wrestling with it. Ratings are based on probability of default; yet they can become irrelevant under short-term stress – look what happened to ratings on banks like Wachovia, going from boom to bust very quickly. Probability of default (PD) based on credit risk may need adjustment in the future regime. Liquidity and the probability of a loss in market confidence may need to become a greater factor; banks are different from corporates. Similarly, ratings based on credit risk alone fail to inform users of potential ratings volatility – especially at the highest ratings. Would PD and a volatility factor be a potential solution? This is something that rating agencies themselves and international regulatory bodies are discussing right now.

Fellow regulator Tom Huertas of the FSA makes a significant point:

Their business model assumed privileged access to information from companies so they could make better judgements about creditworthiness – a semi-insider status. But they failed with securitized obligations and structured finance. They had a good model but one that was built off this framework of privileged access. We may need a different approach for structured products.

Former rating agency head Robin Monro-Davies suggests a return to common sense for the agencies:

The agencies certainly contributed to the bubble. What's the solution? Use common sense and bright people. One lesson: if you need higher maths to steer ratings, you probably shouldn't do it. When stress occurs, models don't work. Look at LTCM (Long Term Credit Management) in the 1990s, whose losses were peanuts compared to sub-prime. Maths overruled common sense. You can look at the history of correlations, but does it sound sensible to get an AAA rating from a lower one? Regulators love ratings but trash rating agencies; it's deep in the culture!

So what is the future of agencies? Two comments from our interviewees look to the possible outcomes. Senior bank analyst Richard Ramsden of Goldman Sachs sums up a common view:

They must be part of the solution. There needs to be a source of information to give investors a sense of risk differentials. They became too close to issuers – a conflict of interest, and the result was pro-cyclical. The whole relationship has to change. The whole system is discredited. And there's little correlation between actual market prices (of CDS) and the ratings on these firms.

A final word comes from a senior investment banker:

There are two problems: they have the wrong methodology, and there's a major conflict of interest. It can't be right to pay agencies to get a rating when the agency is run to make money. The solution: you have to become a public service or lose it (your role) to the market. CDS spreads are a better indicator now than the rating and they're real!

4
The Lessons for Future Risk Management

While top management must take ultimate responsibility for risk management as the previous chapter confirms, they still need better tools and processes for the future.

The role of statistical models

One of these tools is risk modelling and allowance for unexpected outcomes.

A veteran investment banker and now bank consultant, Jim Freeman of Freeman & Co in NY, points out the weaknesses in statistical models for derivative products:

> Process has run ahead of the capability of people running risk management. It's happened again and again since derivatives have become a major part of position management. Starting in the 1970s, people have never understood the secondary effects of the derivatives we create and package. We have to be more cautious! For example, in the US market crash of 1987, investors used what was termed 'portfolio insurance' to cover their risks – a link between index funds and the cash market – but it created a downward spiral of selling.

> We create things that blow ourselves up. We're willing to chase profits before we fully understand the ramifications of derivatives.

Vasco Moreno, the Co-CEO of Keefe Bruyette & Woods Ltd, an investment bank that specializes in the financial services sector, expresses a similar view:

> You need to throw out the risk tools they teach at business school, like VAR (value at risk) models. Risk models need to incorporate very improbable events and they need to better reflect systematic risk.

John Leonard, a career bank stock analyst and fund manager at BlackRock Investment Management in London, agrees:

> We have to be reminded of 'tail' events – lots of financial transactions don't have a normal statistical distribution. For example, in mortgages, a 10 basis point loss ratio may be average, but it could be 50 bp and a worst case scenario could be 90 bp – i.e. a long tail – and it could even be a meteorite!

> We also have to question the stability of the models used by regulators and rating agencies. In the UK, regulators in late 2008 moved the goal posts by stress testing a worst case and told the banks 'your capital is inadequate' even though there was no change in the business. We also need to question the assumption of a normal, liquid market – i.e. that you can buy and sell at a 'fair' price. In retrospect, lots of selling in the crisis has been due to the heavily leveraged 'carry trade'. And finally, as the Spanish regulator has done, we need to view provisions across the cycle. Growth in volume should be reflected in comparable provision levels.

The role of risk management and experience

As indicated below and in the previous chapter, the quality of a bank's risk management itself accounts for much of the damage from the credit crisis. The lack of deep risk management experience at the top of the bank, delegation of key risk decisions to technical specialists, and expansion into unfamiliar products and markets overwhelmed the leadership of many banks.

For Andy Maguire,

> The key is to stop when you get out of your circle of competence, then regulators should take action.

A senior investment banker is outspoken on the subject:

> There are so many multiple risks in play – globality, securitization, etc – and all these are being taken without a risk manager at the top. Banks' big problem is that they have committed themselves to risk taking, but the individuals who run them, using questionable models like VaR, have to deal with complexities far beyond their grasp, and delegate it to technical people.

Sam Theodore, who had spent over 15 years managing European bank ratings, first at Moody's and then at DBRS, notes that a transformation of risk management has been driven by the recent crisis:

> The whole mentality is changing for banks and investors. Credit risk transfer in the 1990s and early 2000s (to off-balance sheet vehicles) was attractive for banks as they had the belief that they had shed credit risk. But much of it was re-intermediated by banks (in many instances not to the originating banks). This is how US sub-prime mortgages ended up in many European banks' books even if they had no direct involvement in the US mortgage market. The danger was amplified by mark-to-market accounting, as these structured-credit securities lost market value as the crisis hit (unlike underlying mortgages which benefit from accrual accounting treatment).

> In addition, banks thought they would save money by cutting back research and using rating agencies, forgetting that they need in-house experts who understand risk and assume responsibility for their research. It is not a responsible approach to delegate crucial credit and investment decisions to third parties like rating agencies, with their mixed track record. Ratings should be a second opinion and nothing more. It is good news that Basel II will be supplemented with an incremental risk charge for market risk, which

will discourage excessive market risk taking and dealing with risky counterparties.

In their efforts to minimize their capital base, banks also focused on their key Tier 1 ratio at the expense of others such as total equity/assets or leverage. Simon Samuels views this as one of the key issues driving the turmoil:

> There was a myopic focus in Europe on a single number – Tier 1 capital ratio – which drove management behaviour. There should have been a more holistic approach with multiple metrics such as used in the US. The heavy reliance on a leverage ratio drove assets off the balance sheet.

Finally, our interviewees focused on the need to align risk with compensation formulae. Newspaper headlines focus on levels of compensation – especially when public funds are at stake – as well as payouts to top management who have not performed. But effective risk management demands alignment between risk takers and their compensation. Former investment banker Jim Freeman is outspoken on the subject:

> The mark-to-market nature of transactions has a secondary effect. Dealers have to mark positions to market. If you have a five year tail (final maturity) to mark, there's no 'cheat box' where you can allow for that risk, so you show a big profit in year one when all the profit is booked. This has to end! People get paid on that profit, not over the five years. You risk paying out short term for a long term risk.

Simon Samuels agrees:

> There's an extraordinary tension between short term profit maxi-mization and long term value – as in the sub prime investments. You need a mechanism to align short and long term at the coal face, such as compensation away from the transaction and based on the lifetime of the product. But for senior management, you have to be humble in your expectations! CEOs are normal peo-ple and it's simply unrealistic to expect them to happily turn

down short term profit opportunities, especially when they have demanding shareholders.

The role of the bank regulator

Finally, what do our interviewees think about the role of the bank regulators in the turmoil? Could they have done a better job in mitigating the damage?

One senior European regulator admits that the outcomes did not reflect well on bank regulation:

> We're on record as having made mistakes. We could have done better – specifically errors of omission. We were victims of our own success. We have to be on top of things. Capital regulations are similar to a covenant in a loan agreement. At some point, if they don't make it, you have to put them into enforcement – and take action. In the past, if a bank failed, we considered it as supervisory failure.

Richard Ramsden is more charitable:

> How could regulation have been improved? It's difficult to answer. There was no victim when everything was going well. Everyone benefited from the system: there was more credit for business, risk was distributed, etc – everyone seemed to benefit, so the regulators were not overly intrusive. They could have looked at concentration of risk in individual banks, or the differential application of accounting rules. But it's not simple to see what they could have done differently.

Santander's Matias Inciarte, however, lauds the relatively pro-active approach of his regulator, the Bank of Spain, which has emerged in the public view with honour from the damage:

> The problem is not *regulation*, but the absence of *supervision*. The Bank of Spain told banks to consolidate SIVs, for example, and other regulators didn't. Before the crisis, we were all wondering where there could be problems. Where? The answer is that it's easy for the regulator to talk to the major banks and ask them if they

see something of concern. That's what the Bank of Spain has done; they have more than 50 supervisors in our bank at any one time looking at what we're doing.

A senior bank rating executive points up the difficulty for regulators to evaluate the critical dimension of liquidity:

Liquidity is important for maintaining confidence, but it's the hardest to predict or measure. Lehman had liquidity but when the problems hit, it didn't matter. If there are no transactions, you're dead! The reality is that you can never hold enough liquidity.

In Chapter 9 we revisit these views and opine on the likelihood of such measures driving behaviour in the future.

5
The Evolution of Business Models

Management oversight and processes for risk management clearly demand significant change in many banks. But is the same true for the business model – a bank's unique blend of product range, client base and geographic focus, together with the related issues of size and complexity?

This chapter addresses specific issues relevant for decisions on a bank's future business model: the issue of size and complexity, the outlook for restructuring by M & A, the key dimensions of the model (geography, client and product), the possible role of regulators in driving the decision on future models, and the perceived views of investors on the appropriate model.

The issue of size and complexity

Prior to the turmoil of 2007–2009, many analysts and consultants argued that banks were becoming too big to manage effectively and that the complexity associated with size actually reduced stockholder value – as well as made such banks 'too big to fail' in a crisis.

Thus a Citigroup research report in 2006 prepared by Simon Samuels and his colleagues concluded that there was a negative correlation between the key stockholder value metrics and the physical size of major European banks – except for a positive one in the metric of CEO compensation! Management of such large banks argued that the economies of scale – particularly in a global retail network – provided an offset to the issue of complexity, and they continued to expand organically and by acquisition.

The advent of the current banking crisis provides support for both points of view. On the one hand, many banking institutions will divest or shrink businesses either because of the need to de-lever and de-risk the portfolio, a perceived need to simplify the business, or to exit a marginal activity. On the other, size has attracted public capital support in markets across the globe as governments seek to refloat their economies and financial sectors. In effect, being 'too big to fail' has been a boon to some troubled banks which otherwise might have been merged out of existence or simply closed down.

Our interviewees provide some contrasting yet penetrating views on the subject!

Perhaps the most interesting is that of Citigroup, regarded by many as the poster child of the downside of size and complexity. Former Chairman Sir Win Bischoff explains the dilemma:

> At Citi, as in other large companies, there is embedded lots of complexity. At the same time, the universal model is now the global model. We're just about the largest of the true universal banks. Our experience has been that growing size leads to more complexity. We're cutting back to around 300,000 employees; it's an awful lot of people, but hopefully the average quality improves.
>
> Yet it's more difficult to have a real entrepreneurial culture with that size in banking. The more management structure there is, the less entrepreneurial you are likely to be. And the ROE is less in a larger, complex structure than in an entrepreneurial one. Additionally it is tough to find good leaders who can manage the cultural differences, for example, between investment banking and retail banking.

But Stephen Green of HSBC, the direct rival to Citi as a global institution, makes a cogent counter-argument:

> There's greater management challenge with size and diversity, but now size and diversity show their strength in a time of turmoil. HSBC is relatively advantaged now with its greater capital strength and business breadth. And we've changed our model in recent years with a focus on emerging markets and connectivity within

the group. For example private banking in Switzerland has a big opportunity in the Middle East.

Vasco Moreno goes much further:

> In the past, small and focused was beautiful; now it's big and diversified. The winning business model has changed 180 degrees as the wholesale funding markets closed. The specialist bank like Northern Rock or consumer finance company has ceased to exist. Now a large bank like Santander is a winner due to low cost of funding and geographic and business line diversification.
>
> In Europe, with the government recapitalizations, the law of natural selection has disappeared; most if not all will survive! Losers will he protected, even if their shareholders are not. This means that transformational banking mergers are unlikely to happen in the medium term.

For Tom Hill of UBS, though, size and complexity remain a central issue in banking:

> This is one of the most important issues today for the industry. Systems and process spread the costs but make it more difficult to understand what's really happening in the customer relationships. It's the challenge of banking: you try to capture economies of scale, but at the same time you find it more and more difficult to know what is going on. In the future, companies will try to become somewhat smaller and less complex – at least until the lessons of this crisis are forgotten and they want to expand again.

A senior executive at Crédit Suisse, UBS' rival, notes the problems facing CS' One Bank policy which calls for collaboration between its wealth management and investment banking businesses.

> It sounds like a good idea. You have, say, 5000 semi-institutional clients in the two businesses so you can do transactions in-house and sell each other's products The problem is in articulating organisational boundaries. Analysts don't trust the model; it's artificial. The result is that investment banking focuses on private banking clients. But you don't need One Bank to make the offer.

What creates value? Look at the relative price/earning ratios. (with wealth management far superior to investment banking)!

For regulator and former rating agency head Sam Theodore,

It's too early to tell which model will win. But there are trends. The market may fear banks that are too big and all-inclusive, but regardless of size they should have clearly defined business lines, with a transparent and simple structure. The 'originate and hold' model is replacing the 'originate and distribute' one. Investment banks won't disappear, but they'll be smaller, and the market will have more difficulties accepting independent investment banks which are of systemic importance – with the power of serious systemic disruption if they get in real trouble. In traditional banking the trend is for a simple business model – providing loans and deposits. Using wholesale funds to fill a gap between the two will be less of a key strategy than before the crisis.

For strategist Robert Albertson, the trends are in the wrong direction:

It's an enigma! The large banks are getting larger and creating yet more systemic risk. We're going in the wrong direction in the US – toward a European model of the universal bank combining investment and retail banking but less innovative than the US model. Look at what happened in Ireland and Spain with the universal model. There's too much concentration in the US and no chance of reducing it. Three banks have 30% of US banking assets; the next layer down will have to take on problem acquisitions. There are some 500–1000 US banks with a CAMEL (risk) rating of four to five (the bottom of the scale) who will need to be bought out or taken over, thus increasing concentration even more.

Another US analyst, Eileen Fahey of Fitch Ratings, takes a more philosophical view:

You can't say now that size is a factor. Greater consolidation has taken place as a result of the crisis. In 1989 the top five US banks had only 15% of US banking assets; in 2008 they have over 60%. There are two aspects of complexity: complexity of the institution in terms of deposit base and breadth of business base; and complexity of product – especially those sold to clients. When regulators played a major role in merging Bank of America and Merrill Lynch, size and complexity were not the issue.

Mark Garvin, International Chairman of JPMorgan Treasury & Securities Services, works for one of the world's largest banks and sees no reason why his bank's size would change its strategy:

> Size is not an issue if the institution is well managed with the right people in leadership positions. Large institutions are not necessarily too risky by dint of their size. J. P. Morgan has six lines of business and is very focussed on managing risk and creating value for shareholders. In 2008 we bought two distressed firms (WaMu and Bear Stearns) and have proven our capacity to integrate both by putting them on our existing platforms.

Banking consultant Andy Maguire goes beyond the pure issue of size and scale:

> The real issue is scale by market – having a small number of large positions. Size itself is not sufficient; it's the franchise footprint.

The outlook for restructuring by M & A

A related issue to that of size and complexity is likely consolidation via the merger and acquisition route as a result of the current turmoil. Historically, such a period creates winners and losers as well as the opportunity to reshape the business model. To date, the great bulk of M & A deals have taken the form of strong taking over weak or failing banks, often with government encouragement and financial support. Thus in the UK, Belgium, the US and other markets public funds have facilitated in 2008 the takeover of institutions as diverse as Merrill Lynch, Fortis Bank, HBOS and Wachovia.

The views of our interviewees on the outlook for additional deals – especially voluntary ones between relatively healthy banks – are as mixed as those above on the issue of size and complexity.

The future role of government as a stockholder is a key driver in the views of many interviewees. In most major markets like the US and the UK, the common view is that governments are not interested in remaining stockholders beyond the period needed to restore financial health. But the precondition for receiving government support in markets like Ireland is an indication of possible future conflicts, as discussed in Chapter 9.

Simon Samuels expresses a thoughtful view on the overall M & A outlook:

> It's hard to say how M & A will evolve. As usual, it depends on the stakeholders. There are two key dimensions: structural and cyclical. The structural driver will remain: CEOs want to grow! In the cyclical dimension, there will clearly be more rescues where a good bank buys a bad one. In this context, the role of a government stockholder is critical. For example, it will be tougher to buy overseas banks or grow internationally for a bank with such a stockholder. Now there is a maximum of uncertainty over asset values so that a buyer may calculate the net present value of a weak bank (like Washington Mutual in the US) at zero and insist on government help.

Jim Freeman echoes this uncertainty:

> There have been no strategic mergers during the crisis; they've all been shotgun. In 2009 there will be the divestiture of bad assets. In the US there are too many large players at the top, and midsized banks will have to acquire to gain critical mass. In 2010 there should be a spirited M & A business!

Sam Theodore, ex-manager of European bank ratings, offers an interesting perspective on post-crisis deals:

> M & A will continue but using different criteria. In the past, it was driven by synergies which were promoted by investors, such as the RBS consortium takeover of ABN AMRO. Now investors no longer pursue such avenues; they aim for safety, not for risk. There will be more systemic consolidation driven by system clean-up dynamics. National champions are again in fashion. The problem will be mid-sized and small banks. Even if confidence returns in general,

it may not, for some time, for such banks that are off the radar screen.

John Leonard of BlackRock expresses a widespread view on the outlook for bank consolidation:

> Is there comparability in governments' approach to bank ownership? There are several approaches: activist with an agenda, a long term stockholder, and short term profit maximization. We'll see them all! In the US at least, management is reluctant to do deals when the economic downside is unclear. Wells Fargo gambled in buying Wachovia. But if the economy shows signs of bottoming, you'll see action. A buyer shouldn't make the first call; you'll get a better price if you are called!

Several interviewees pointed to the massive uncertainties in executing M & A in the current environment. The debacle of Merrill's unexpected losses on the Bank of America transaction is on the minds of many. Andy Maguire points out that

> Big deals like Wachovia/Wells Fargo can make you or break you. Who knows what you'll find in the mortgages they bought? You can talk about due diligence until you're blue in the face, but you just don't KNOW how deals will work out. It's all about survival!

There is, however, general consensus that simplicity and focus will be key benchmarks in future banking structures. Thus Roberto Nicastro notes that

> A positive impact of the crisis for UniCredit will be more focus. There's a demand for more simplicity and selectivity and away from the financial supermarket. In the consolidation process there are two contradictory trends: more bank failures and sales, but on the other hand banks will have to focus on the basics like customer service and stability – the soft values, rather than M & A.

Another senior European banker, Matias Inciarte of Santander, agrees:

> We'll see a significant decline in complexity of activities. Invest-
> ment banking, as well as trading activities, will suffer for a long
> time. There will be a retreat to traditional commercial banking
> activities – but at much higher margins.

A senior executive of Deutsche Bank adds that

> There will be a trend toward middle-sized banks. Some deals will
> be undone – those which aren't yet integrated. It's easier to sell off
> units that aren't really integrated. The key is not product but size
> of retail footprint.

A final word comes from consultant Charles Wendel:

> Our clients are asking 'how does a business support our core
> mission'. They will pull back in product, client segment and
> geography – essentially 'narrow down' – at least for the next five
> years. Banks weren't narrow enough. But they still haven't decided
> what businesses they want to be in!

The regulators' views as a driver of bank strategic models

Most of our interviewees identified the future posture of bank regulators as a major driver of business models and strategy. Likely decisions
on bank capital and liquidity, acceptable levels of risk and the views
of individual national regulators – all play a significant role in how
bank management are shaping their business models. At the time of
writing, such regulatory guidance is widely viewed as uncertain in
detail but broadly accepted in outline. For example, it is generally
understood by bank management that Basel II will be replaced by
'Basel III' which will address some of the weaknesses of its predecessor, but bankers know that it took some nine years to shape Basel II,
and even now the US does not subscribe to it in detail.

Given these caveats, however, management must be setting the
broad guidelines now for their future strategy, and the following
comments are useful in profiling the likely management responses.

A widespread concern of bank management is the likely impact of government ownership and political involvement on the regulatory environment. A senior executive of a major European banking group with deep commitments in several national markets opines off the record as follows:

> There's a temptation for government to have a Colbertian (the former French minister known for his mercantilist views) approach to control banks to follow their economic policies. Some like the UK will be liberal; the government will exit in better times. Germany is the worst for relinquishing control, with Italy and France in between. I'm concerned: we risk becoming a public utility. It will generally increase differentiation by country; each one will have a different approach, which will make it harder to run the business.

A senior investment banker with decades of experience in the London market views with concern the likely increased cost of regulation and its impact on bank strategies:

> The big danger from regulation is that it becomes too costly to maintain and administer, which gives a premium to size. If you're small, it becomes too expensive to administer. The gap between strong and weak will grow.

A senior executive from Deutsche Bank is also concerned about the cost of regulation, this time for a major bank with national operations across the globe:

> In the short term, the crisis will make it extremely complex. Everyone is looking at some aspect of regulation. In the long term, regulation will be simpler – a trend toward commonality of regulation – maybe merging of regulators, or maybe more single regulators who supervise the totality of a bank.

For many banks, the relative capital required for relatively risky businesses like investment banking as opposed to low risk deposit-based business like retail banking will be a key driver of their future business model.

McKinsey's Pat Butler has thought creatively about the choice:

While the G30 has set out the broad agenda for regulation, it is the details yet to be defined that will shape the business models of banks.

So for instance regulators might choose to tackle the 'too big to fail' problem by imposing additional costs on large complex financial institutions that may make simpler business models more attractive. They could go further and regulate in favour of 'narrow banking', arguing that commercial banking and investment banking should not combine in a world where the taxpayer pays for failure.

Capital levels is another regulatory issue that will shape business models; while everyone agrees that banks need to hold more capital, the real question is how much more and in what form. If the issue is genuine 'tail-risk', the solution may be access to capital on more of an insurance basis – just as you would ensure your house against the risk of lightning. This could be in the form of debt that would convert if a specific event occurred or contingent access to pools of capital for which you pay an insurance premium.

On the systemic risk front, while there is much talk of macro-prudential supervision, regulators may want to slow down the pace of new product innovation. New products like CDOs spread like viruses across the banking world. Regulators could slow this down by requiring all products over a certain volume to be exchange traded or at least go through a clearing house.

There may also be a move by investors away from the large complex financial conglomerates that they could not understand. They may push for much greater investor clarity – 'I'll do my own diversification, thank you'.

For a senior investment banker, the likely outcome is clear:

Risk taking will have to be a relatively small portion of the total strategy – regulators will see to that! If you are in the public market and you run big risks, the stockholders will leave you. You can't run a casino and take mega risks – it's OK as a partnership but not with other people's money.

How might the three elements of the business model evolve?

Business models reflect choices among three key dimensions: product range, client segments and geographic scope. We examine below the impact of the turmoil on each one. In sum, there are components which are widely regarded as more attractive post-turmoil, some which are less so, and others which are viewed as unchanged.

Product range

The unanimous view of our interview sample is that deposit taking from a customer base should be the dominant product priority in an environment where sources of wholesale funds have virtually dried up and, at best, will be substantially reduced in the longer term. In the retail world, the phrases 'back to basic banking', 'traditional loans and deposits' and 'plain vanilla banking' are top of mind.

Simon Samuels expresses the universal view that customer deposits should drive the business model for a commercial bank:

> Focus on the liability side of the balance sheet, not investment banking or consumer credit. Go for people's savings! Securitization will not return in importance: two-thirds of the buyers (SIVs, conduits and hedge funds) have largely gone.

Robert Albertson agrees:

> There's a big reversal of sentiment on fee income: it's no longer the golden egg! Spread income from credit products will be key, not the capital markets. Efforts will be made to improve customer relationships by cross selling, but there's been only glacial progress on that to date.

Vasco Moreno focuses not just on this priority for funding purposes but also for profitability:

Simple retail banking strategies will be very profitable for the next two years. Retail deposits are very cheap and they allow the banks to lend to prime borrowers at very high spreads. Mortgage spreads of 150–300 basis points over Treasuries, earning a reasonable ROE on low loan to value loans... we have not had these retail banking product spreads for over 15 years.

We found mixed views on the attractiveness of wealth management (for High Net Worth individuals) and the asset management product. Most of our interviewees agree with John Leonard that diversified banks should

Focus on fee-earning markets with critical mass, like wealth management, asset management and retirement savings, despite their cyclical nature. Traditional products like trade finance and transaction services should produce good scale economies. But the big lesson of the crisis is not to concentrate on a narrow lending business line (as did Northern Rock in the UK and Anglo Irish in Ireland). If you have to add capital for a worst case scenario, the result will be so extreme that the cost of capital will offset the return.

Among the global, diversified banks, Sir Win Bischoff of Citi gives high priority to wealth management and cash management:

We'll focus on traditional banking – products like global cash management, which is our only business whose earnings have not fallen much in this cycle, and wealth management with its lower capital cost.

Charles Wendel adds:

There will be a focus on treasury services and cash management to accumulate a deposit base. Wealth management is especially attractive with an aging customer base which doesn't borrow and has liquidity.

The likely increase in savings rates in markets like the US and the UK provides added impetus to such a deposit-gathering strategy. Richard Ramsden notes that

> Savings rates will increase dramatically; banks will focus on the liability side of the balance sheet. There will be fewer products but priced correctly. Less innovation is more!

The importance of product pricing is also emphasized by Andy Maguire:

> The key is to reprice the asset book; pricing got a little silly in the boom period. Decide who you want to extend credit to and get rid of the 'capital hogs'. Deposits are good to have but banks risk paying over the odds for them and then losing them – a double whammy! Wealth management is not the way forward for the broad mass of banks – it's a small segment for most – but if you've got it, flaunt it!

In contrast, many diversified banks are exiting the asset management sector. Two leading French banks, Société Générale and Crédit Agricole, have merged their fund management businesses as a partial step in this direction. Crédit Suisse sold its traditional asset management business at year-end 2008, while Tom Hill at Swiss rival UBS agrees that

> On the whole, banks make bad owners of asset management firms; there are only a few exceptions, where the investors are truly autonomous.

In sharp contrast, there is widespread agreement that investment banking, as practised prior to mid-2007, is the least attractive business for a diversified banking group. The sharp cyclical downturn in client transactions, the shrinkage of core client segments such as hedge funds and private equity, the virtual disappearance of members of the 'shadow banking' sector – all lead to the conclusion that the sector will generate modest returns at best over the intermediate term. Banks like Crédit Suisse are focusing on acting as agent rather than risking capital; Crédit Suisse for one has reported that such a strategy would have generated a profit in 2008 for the investment bank rather than the loss reported.

Yet Goldman Sachs, the archetype of the 'monoline' investment bank, will not change its core strategy. Managing Director Lucas Van Praag reports that

> Goldman's business model is unchanged; we'll focus on the advisory role and co-investing (in sectors such as private equity and distressed debt). Our ROTE target is unchanged since our flotation in 1999 – 20% over the cycle.

We profile Goldman's strategy in Chapter 8 as a case study of successful focus on a single global segment – in the much criticized sector of investment banking!

Client segments

Client segments differ in size of client, wealth, sophistication, nature of product demand and a host of other variables. Given the strategic product priority of customer deposits indicated above, it is understandable that those segments which may yield a rich harvest of such deposits – affluent and wealthy individuals, small and medium enterprises (SME) who generate positive cash flows, institutional investors and others – have been assigned priority status as a result of the current turmoil. Our research into the affluent and high net worth segments indicates, for example, that perhaps a quarter of such client revenues are comprised of traditional loan and deposit revenues.

As Vasco Moreno points out,

> A model with a focus on deposit gathering is simple and can generate terrific risk-adjusted returns. You don't need to be too sophisticated.

Eileen Fahey of Fitch agrees:

> High net worth should still be a focus; go for the client with the cash! And you need to grow your deposit base. Do you need more branches to develop a personal relationship with the client? But at the same time you need to cut costs via electronic delivery.

Another attractive segment includes core processing businesses like cash management, trade finance, securities processing and others which demand relatively little capital but produce positive cash flow, regular fee income and significant economies of scale.

A global bank like HSBC or Citigroup is a natural home for a range of individual, institutional and corporate clients requiring a global service capability. As Sir Win Bischoff explains,

> Citi doesn't have a national branch network in the US, so we have to go for the top 2,000 companies and leverage our global reach. And you need to be in the local market to do SME well.

For an investment bank like Goldman Sachs, corporations who need refinancing represent an attractive opportunity. Lucas Van Praag sees a host of opportunities for Goldman:

> We're focusing on distressed debt investing. Equity markets are also attractive, as are recapitalisations of financial institutions, asset management, prime brokerage in a dislocating market, foreign exchange and commodities, advice to sovereign entities, as well as credit and interest rate products.

One of our interviewees also points out that

> Goldman has a small number of very wealthy and powerful clients; it could be the largest private bank in the world! Goldman is a merchant bank for these clients – not institutional asset management but a private bank. Other investment banks will try to do the same.

Geographic focus

At the outset of the current banking turmoil, emerging markets from the Central and Eastern Europe (CEE) to Asia-Pacific to Latin America were the almost universal geographic priority for banks largely because of their superior growth potential. Economic growth in most of the developed world had shrunk to low single digits, and competition had slashed margins across the board.

While emerging markets have suffered during the current crisis, our interviewees largely agree that the crisis, broadly speaking, had actually enhanced the value of a strong position in these growth markets. The principal caveat has been a more selective approach to individual emerging markets.

A typical response comes from HSBC's Stephen Green:

The turmoil has reinforced our view that Asia will outgrow the US.

Sir Win Bischoff of Citigroup notes that

Citi wants to shift from 60% in US earnings to 60% in non-US, particularly in the emerging markets. The key for us is ubiquity in these markets – a terrific strategy.

Adds Jim Freeman:

South east Asia – in particular China – is the US of the current century!

A thoughtful response comes from Simon Samuels:

The classic response is for banks to run from one side of the boat to the other in a crisis, but in the case of growth markets the arguments are even stronger now: long term economic growth, positive demographics, and level of banking penetration. There will be problems in the short term in some countries, but the overall concept of emerging markets is valid.

When asked what strategic changes have taken place for Goldman Sachs in the past few years, the answer from Lucas Van Praag is clear:

Our business focus is much more global – in particular in the BRIC (Brazil, Russia, India and China) countries. We've obtained licenses and built businesses in all four in the last two years. To do so we've pulled in people from all over the world – tested Goldman people. Our strategy is to invest in people and licenses in these growth areas.

But Tom Hill of UBS adds a key caveat:

> Banks will focus on emerging markets on a case by case basis, not emerging markets as a whole. Russia is not China. You can't say 'all emerging markets are OK.'

John Leonard adds:

> Emerging markets are important, but you need to look for economic and financial stability as well as growth during the next few years.

A senior executive of Deutsche Bank echoes this more cautious approach:

> Many banks will shift resources away from the emerging markets. The speed of expansion there will lessen in favour of home markets like the US and Europe. Emerging markets were 'the icing on the cake' – not a major portion of the balance sheet.

A major theme of our conversations was the need to focus more resources on the home market – both for economic and political reasons. The latter theme is very much on the minds of banks in markets where the taxpayer has pumped massive resources into the banking system.

Thus Sam Theodore points out that

> The strategy of a large universal bank should have as an anchor the home market. This will give credibility, stability, predictability, while increasing the systemic importance vis-à-vis the government.

Matias Inciarte echoes this view, but with a critical caveat:

> There's a trend now to retreat to the home market, both to solve problems and to de-leverage. But that misses the point. You need diversity. Look at Spain, which is in a serious recession with negative growth. But with Latin America we have sustained growth. A lesson from the crisis is that diversity is the key, but only if you have competitive advantage in the other markets.

A final point is made by Richard Ramsden in evaluating the results in the US of banks expanding outside their home base:

> One mistake made by US banks is 'out of footprint' lending. Look at the performance – much worse than lending to people you know! The good news is that banks can now afford to pick and choose as well as demand a larger margin.

The investor model

To judge from the public posture, what the investor now wants from buying bank stocks is quite straightforward. Banks must de-lever, de-risk, and become more transparent and simple in business model. In sharp contrast, the old model before mid-2007 was quite different: maximize ROE – up to 20% or more, increase annual earnings growth by a double digit amount, ideally from organic expansion rather than acquisitions, and meet the earnings guidance regularly handed out by management.

The result has been a well-advertised collapse of performance metrics across the board, with little discrimination between those who meet the new criteria and those who do not. This poses some obvious questions. First, what happened to earnings growth as an objective? Do investors want a return to the situation decades ago when banks were viewed as public utilities with a reliable dividend stream? Will the new model endure over time when the next boom period occurs? The views of our interviewee sample are interesting!

Matias Inciarte expresses a common view:

> We're in a period of maximum instability. There are no objective measures. Investors have lost confidence in bank figures. Numbers mean nothing. The market doesn't appreciate good results. We need a period of stability and transparency – time – before there's any model.

Roberto Nicastro agrees:

> Investors are pretty scared. What will happen in two years? If we try to do anything to move away from the short term, like dropping quarterly reporting, we'd get killed by the analysts. But in practice our business model will be more focused.

Andy Maguire takes a more cynical view:

> The current view will change! It's not de-leveraging, but higher growth and returns will be targeted. It is a natural progression to yet higher targets. It's the nature of the world, and there should not be any illusions about what will happen next time.

On the other hand, Richard Ramsden takes investors at their word:

> The root cause (of the crisis) was the growth model. Banks were pushed to grow faster than GDP in mature markets, which led to leverage and prioritising high margin products. Things will now go into reverse; growth rates will be tied to GDP.

Pulling it all together!

Reviewing these comments provides a useful profile of current strategic wisdom but at the same time raises a number of key points which will be discussed further in the concluding Chapter 9.

First, selecting the desired mix of client, product and geography is only the first step in the strategic process. Our goal in this book is to identify durable strategies that will stand the test of time, and other ingredients must be added to the recipe for success. For example, we have already studied the risk management dimension in the preceding chapter. Thus, one cannot evaluate Goldman Sach's strategy without assessing its remarkable risk management skills in a volatile business.

Another key variable is that of soft skills – in particular leadership and culture, which will be examined in the next chapter. This chapter has identified such skills as a critical ingredient of the strategies of the massive global banks like HSBC and Citigroup.

Third is the issue of timing. As Simon Samuels points out, in a crisis banks tend to move from one side of the boat to the other. Two years ago the monoline model in mortgage lending, consumer finance and credit insurance was all the rage; today it is virtually dead. Today deposit gathering has dominated management thinking, but as markets and economies recover, in a few years competition for such customer funding may well reduce margins well below those needed to sustain a double digit ROE.

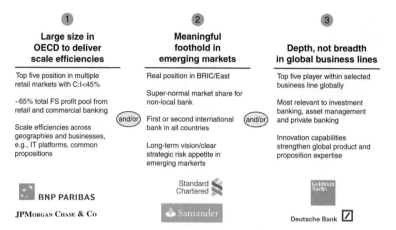

Figure 5.1 What might a winning portfolio look like
Source: The Boston Consulting Group – International Bank Planners Forum Presentation, November 2008.

A tentative conclusion from this chapter is that there is no magic, ideal business model for the long term. Yet one can certainly identify models which are more likely to succeed than others. Chapter 8 profiles case studies of these successful models which might provide a template for other banks.

This chapter concludes with Figure 5.1 from BCG which suggests three macro-strategic approaches for the post-turmoil world: major banks in developed market with size and scale; those with strength in attractive emerging markets, and banks with depth globally in core businesses like investment banking and wealth management.

While opinions will certainly differ on the examples cited in each case by BCG – and our selection in Chapter 8 provides some other choices – the underlying segmentation approach is a sensible one. Our final chapter provides our own conclusions on the way forward! Readers will note that three of BCG's examples – Standard Chartered Bank, Santander and Goldman Sachs – are included in Chapter 8. In contrast, Bank of America and Lloyds TSB, while success stories prior to the crisis, each became a case study of defective execution with their mergers (Merrill Lynch and HBOS) during the crisis – yet another example of the dangers of forecasting during the turmoil.

6
The Role of Leadership and Culture

Before focusing on the role of leadership and culture in the current banking crisis, it might be useful to take a few steps backwards to put these variables in the context of our research on the subject going back to the mid-1990s.

Leadership in Financial Services (Macmillan, 1997) was written in the years following the great wave of mergers which created today's major banks: the two global Swiss institutions, HSBC, Citigroup, BNP Paribas, Wells Fargo, JPMorgan and others who dominate today's league tables. The core leadership challenge then was to blend the cultures – defined simply as 'how we do things here', often from totally different markets and traditions – and create a single institution with common values, systems and financial goals. A quotation from our earlier 1989 book on excellence in banking on the leadership challenge was still valid in 1997:

> The guidelines are reasonably clear. Select and drive home the values that can unite an increasingly diverse team. Support entrepreneurship but ensure that some form of discipline is a cherished value. Place an even higher priority of communication and honesty in addressing the stresses which will inevitably arise. Be patient; acknowledge that people take time to adjust to new realities. And make meritocracy one of your values – especially if you want to infuse a traditional organization with young, more talented blood.

Consultants have offered bank management advice in dealing with the inevitable conflicts based on high-level generalizations such as 'loose/tight', 'think globally and act locally'. Yet actually creating a single banking organization facing roughly the same direction has been an ongoing challenge for decades.

The leaders we profiled in 1997 and a subsequent book (*Excellence in Banking Revisited*) in 2004 included success stories of leaders in banking and finance who have stood the test of time: John Whitehead of Goldman Sachs, Emilio Botin of Santander, Dick Kovacevich of Wells Fargo, Alessandro Profumo of UniCredit, and Claude Bebear of AXA. But they also included a few subsequently who fell by the wayside, largely because of problems of risk management, such as Charlie Sanford of Bankers Trust, Marcel Ospel and Peter Wuffli of UBS, and Rolf Hueppi of Zurich Insurance.

Looking back over this research, one conclusion leaps out: risk management was not even mentioned in the 1989 paragraph of core values! While the samples in the research were limited, they did include most of the names of bankers and financiers who were associated at the time with excellence in management.

This brief excursion into banking history thus places in perspective the challenge of the current financial crisis and the dramatic changes which have taken place at the top of some of the world's leading banks. While the past few decades have seen banking crises, the trauma of 2007–2008 was a unique challenge. As Lucas Van Praag noted in our interview for this book,

No one imagined the degree of dislocations in the credit markets.

Many of the leaders who have involuntarily left the scene in 2007–2008 had impressive experience in general management and certainly possessed the 'soft' skills of managing a large and complex bank, but they often lacked the deep risk management experience and judgement which was highlighted in the quotations in Chapter 4. Many of the survivors at the top may have lacked hands-on risk management credentials, but generally they had the judgement, as Stephen Green pointed out in Chapter 4, to avoid risks they couldn't understand.

So how do our interviewees view banking leadership today? The challenge of managing massive and complex organizations remains. Banks still face the need to bring together disparate cultures and practices. At the same time, risk management remains a top priority as the crisis evolves.

One issue raised by our interviews is the adequacy of leadership at the top of banking today.

One of our consultants is outspoken on the topic:

> There aren't enough leaders! Goldman Sachs does it exceptionally well. Jamie Dimon of JPMorgan Chase is extraordinarily good but may have portfolio problems. UBS made the mistake of putting people in charge who didn't know the products.

One of the CEOs interviewed notes that

> At the top of the world's 20–30 banks there are lots of people who are out of jobs as leadership has changed. But you can bring in the right leadership from the outside. The new CEO of RBS has never run a bank before, but [running a bank] is not that mysterious!

Simon Samuels comments that it may be premature to draw conclusions on leadership today:

> Lots can still happen; the crisis isn't over yet. Who has shown the ability (by luck or judgement) to ride out the crisis? Is it JPMorgan, Santander or Wells Fargo? Even though a trillion dollars of subprime loans have been written off, there could be lots more from corporate exposure. For five years HSBC's acquisition of Household Finance in the US was considered a great deal; since then its subprime loans have destroyed a ton of value.

For Sam Theodore, superior leadership has been

> ...basically top management of groups like Santander or Unicredito who didn't fall for the quick fix of high but volatile earnings but kept looking to build an in-franchise strategy.

Tom Hill of UBS links culture with leadership:

> You start with culture. The first risk control is a single employee's decision. If he has to consult the rule book or ask the boss the

whole time, something is wrong. He has to know what the right behaviour is. And culture follows top management behaviour. What do you do when mistakes are made? Who gets promoted? And why?

A positive note is struck by Robert Albertson:

New leadership will emerge from the crisis with a new generation of leaders. There aren't enough of them now. In the US, Wells Fargo and US Bancorp have good leaders, with Goldman Sachs in investment banking.

A senior European banker focuses on the cultural gap between the leaders in a major bank and colleagues who run individual businesses:

There's a clear gap between the top management with a good overview of banking and in touch with the local market environment, and the people who run it at the operating level, who are all motivated by their own area. There's no one there fighting for the good of the firm.

Many of our interviewees were scathing in their evaluation of bank leadership in recent years. One of our senior rating agency executives notes that

We've been suckered by apparently strong leadership in banks like RBS. There'll be a reaction against the charismatic CEO for some time.

A US-based banking consultant goes further:

Is there ANY leadership at the top banks? You can count them on the fingers of one hand. Big banks have big issues – many are run by deal people, not bankers!

A leading bank consultant makes a semi-humorous but telling comment on bank leadership:

There are three schools of thought in categorizing bank leadership. One is the strong individual with years of track record who –

so far – has been successful. The second is a strong individual with a similar long track record whose bank or insurance company has blown up in his face. What's the difference? Is it luck or timing? Five years ago the criterion was longevity; at AIG it took a long time (to blow up)! And the third is the institutional approach, like that at HSBC, where the leadership is part of a dynasty which prepares the bank for the next generation.

Richard Ramsden points out that good leadership is even more important now in the strategic equation:

> The market has pushed bank management to do stupid things that can take 10 years to undo. You avoid that by leadership that has a clear idea on what has to change – not dumb strategies because the market demands that you do something. Good leadership also avoids doing expensive deals at the wrong end of the cycle.

One of the major banks which is widely viewed as having emerged from the crisis relatively unscathed is JPMorgan Chase. Mark Garvin summarizes his view of their performance:

> We've made our share of mistakes but fewer than others! It's like a boxing match: you have to go 15 rounds and still be standing at the last one. We avoided some of the pitfalls that bedevilled our competitors, such as SIVs, and scaled back on sub-prime lending before others did. We will continue to invest in systems and cut costs where we can so we can go another 15 rounds the next time.

7
How Might Future Bank Profits and Returns Evolve?

For a banking meltdown predicted by only a handful of observers, what is now widely viewed as the deepest and longest lasting global downturn since the 1930s has generated a host of forecasts both for the banking system and the global economy in general. This chapter will summarize briefly the efforts by global agencies such as the IMF and bank economists to provide answers to the universal questions of length, depth and profile of the downturn. It will then turn in more detail to the views of our interview sample.

Such forecasts invariably are based on past downturns, in particular those commencing with a banking crisis which is followed by a major economic recession or depression. The widespread assumption, as indicated in Chapter 2, is that such a combination is more lethal than the two downturns occurring separately.

An obvious question is the timing of these prognostications, as well as that of the writing of this book. For a global banking crisis which has confounded all the experts in its unexpected twists and turns, it would appear naïve to build forecasts now which extend into the medium term. This may well prove to be true, but a strong argument can be made now that the major developments in the banking crisis itself have been manifested and that the major unknowns lie in the economic impact of the banking crisis. Those unknowns are clearly important in terms of the potential losses to the banks, but other important variables, such as government support for the banks, have largely been clarified.

Such assumptions rest on the traumatic events of the last few months of 2008, when governments in the major developed and developing markets alike not only committed to pour 'whatever it takes' in taxpayer funds to revive their economies, but also, for the first time in decades, to do the same for their banking systems in the form of billions of dollars equivalent in capital contributions. Thus the quasi-nationalization of major US and UK banks as well as government intervention in other important markets during the market firestorm in October 2008 are landmarks in the evolution of the meltdown.

We return to this central caveat in our forecast in Chapter 9.

A seminal study of historical banking and economic crises in this context is that carried out in late 2008 by the IMF. Its economic team studied 113 different periods of substantial financial stress in the past 30 years in 17 developed markets. One of its core conclusions is that economic recessions preceded by financial stress have been more than twice as long and four times as deep as those without that banking trigger. Thus the average output loss in the former was 19.8% of GDP against 4.1% in the pure economic downturn.

Another approach has been taken by Citigroup's European economic team, which has analysed selected banking crises on a global scale as well as going back much further in time to the US banking and economic collapse of the 1930s, which is used by many economists as the base case for the current crisis. Their sample also includes the subsequent Japanese property bubble and subsequent deflation of the 1990s, the Swedish banking crisis of the early 1990s, and the Hong Kong deflationary period of 1997–2002 following the Asian banking collapse. Citigroup's focus is to record how the banking system coped with such hostile environments and the financial results which might therefore be anticipated in the current one.

One of the most interesting statistical findings of the Citigroup study is the duration and financial impact of these selected banking collapses. Figure 7.1 indicates that the maximum period of banking losses or downturn in profitability was three years, followed by a sharp recovery in profits to previous high levels.

Thus even in the US, where the economic depression continued for a much longer period, bank profits turned negative only during the 1932–1934 period and by 1937 had recovered to the highs of 1929. The US depression drove a massive collapse of bank profits of over

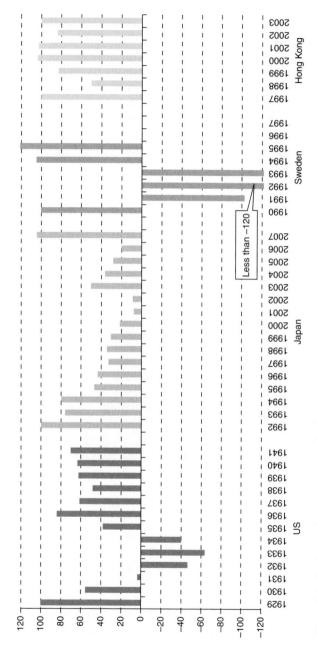

Figure 7.1 Profit trends from previous banking crises (indexed to 100)
Source: Citigroup, Federal Reserve Archives, company data, Riksbank, HKMA.

160% and Swedish banks reported even greater percentage losses. On the other hand, US loan volumes fell by only 50% from peak to trough, and the banks' equity/asset ratio also tumbled by half.

For its sample of European banks, Citigroup concludes that the current downturn will drive a 30–60% decline in its pre-crisis forecasts for banks' gross operating profits, loan volumes and deposit balances. Citi's forecast for the sector's ROE 'through the cycle' is 14% following a massive de-leveraging process, against 18% pre-crisis. Price/book ratios of 1.5 times might be appropriate against pre-crisis ones of 2.5 times.

Our final macro input is a survey of European bank stock investors conducted by Merrill Lynch in December 2008 which, among other things, concluded that the largest proportion – over a third – of these investors forecast an economic recession similar to that of the US in the 1990s (following the savings and loan crisis), with a much lower percentage anticipating a collapse similar to that of the US in the 1930s.

Our interview series generated responses which generally track the findings from these and similar surveys, but at the same time provided more detail and context for their reasoning.

For Jim Freeman,

> In the wholesale/investment banking area, a reasonable ROE is 15% – the same as Sandy Weill's old target for any financial institution with which he was involved, including Citigroup. To reach 20% you need to have a major differentiator!

Simon Samuels echoes Citigroup's research findings for European banks:

> Our normalized profit projections on average work out to 14% – a boring conclusion! Banks thus show the same ROE as for corporates in general. In the past, the ROE figure for banks was 20% plus, but there has been a big change in attitude, and the 14% assumes some years will be lower. And the projected return for investment banks is worst of all!

Sir Win Bischoff is also comfortable with a projected range of 13–15% over the cycle.

Tom Hill of UBS agrees and supplies an interesting rationale:

> In recent years, US bank earnings as a percentage of total US cor-
> porate profits had risen from an average of 20% to 40%. There's
> something wrong with that; banks are essentially intermediaries
> providing finance to the economy; 40% of profits can't make sense
> in the long run. In recent years, apparent higher returns stemmed
> from excess leverage. In future ROEs will revert to the historical
> mean of about 14%.

John Leonard agrees that bank ROEs will fall to a level of 12–15%:

> The banks will need more capital support over the next 3–5 years,
> and also a higher spread over the risk-free rate. So the cost of cap-
> ital will rise. Regulators will limit leverage. The issue is how much
> of that higher spread is passed back to the borrower. There should
> be a seller's market in credit, but the customer relationships will
> dampen pricing. You can look back to 1992–93 crisis in the US
> when the government took loans off the banks' books, and the
> extra deposits led to a collapse of rates and high bank profits. Now
> banks want deposits and are prepared to pay high spreads to build
> their customer deposit base.

For Robert Albertson as well, performance metrics will decline:

> The old business model will be restored over time, with reduced
> leverage and higher loan spreads. An ROE of 10–12% will be the
> norm, and a stronger net interest margin will drive profitability.

Sam Theodore also looks to the past for guidance:

> In the 1980s, a single digit ROE was OK; look at the Swiss and
> German banks of the time. A higher ROE has been obtained
> from leverage and investment banking; it won't come back! The
> same for high volumes of mortgage lending and cheap wholesale
> money. The issue is whether the market will accept it. When the
> crisis eases, what will be the expectations for revenue growth?

Vasco Moreno agrees that

Investors want material deleveraging and more capital allocated to low risk, low return activities. The result will be a lower ROE, perhaps in line with the cost of equity (ie 10–12%). Now banks in Europe are selling at 0.6 times book, thus pricing in even lower ROEs.

Another bank analyst, Richard Ramsden, sees a similar decline:

If you look back to the period between the 1930s and the 1980s in the US, earnings growth was close to that of GDP, but since then it's been a multiple of GDP until 2007. ROE rose dramatically because of increased asset velocity and leverage. We'll go back to the GDP growth rate, with ROEs in the 'teens, not 20s. A lot depends on the regulators!

Eileen Fahey offers some thoughts on the timing of future ROEs:

Provisions will eat up profits until the second quarter of 2009 and then return to more normal levels. ROE will be in the low single digits – say 5–9%, rising to 10–15% in 2010/11 and higher in the long term as banks cut costs.

A somewhat more optimistic view is projected – at least at the current moment – by some of our interviewees. As noted above, Goldman Sachs has maintained unchanged its goal of a 20% ROTE (return on tangible equity) over the cycle, although clearly results will fall below this mark in the short term.

And at HSBC Stephen Green notes that their medium-term target ROE over the cycle – a range between 15% and 19% – has not been modified as a result of the crisis.

Several observers note that the disparity in banks' ROE should widen as a result of the crisis. For example, Roberto Nicastro points out that

Future ROE is the billion dollar question! In any industry there will be less leverage and this translates in to lower net profitability. However I would still expect good banks to achieve double digit ROEs. There will be more differentiation from bank to bank. Being selective by segment could be a more important differentiator.

Consultant Charles Wendel agrees:

> There will be greater differentiation in ROE than in the past. In the US, a leader like Wells Fargo might achieve a level of 18–20%; while lots of banks earning 10–12% ROEs might disappear.

McKinsey's Pat Butler agrees with the consensus 12–15% for most banks, but adds a major caveat:

> Banks will carry more capital and be subject to more regulation, so the result might well be a range of 12–15%. The real worry however is the spectre of deflation as in Japan in the 1990s. Over ten years, Japanese bank revenues fell 66% – a catastrophic collapse – and they still have not recovered. The market pumped liquidity into the system, and indeed hoped for inflation, but the money flowed into US Treasury Bills rather than the banking system of the Japanese economy. You have to accept a 25% probability of that happening again in some of the developed economies.

A final comment comes from a European banker when asked his views on the likely level of ROEs:

> The issue is not the *level* of ROE but whether we have *adequate* capital!

We comment in Chapter 9 on these views in a longer term context.

8
Case Studies of Successful Strategic Models

Previous chapters have set out the lessons learned from the current crisis, business models which should thrive in relative terms in the new environment, the likely profit profile for these models, and the leadership challenge for banks. We now focus more sharply on specific case studies of banks which not only fit this profile, but have also emerged from the turmoil without serious damage to their reputation and profitability.

The primary criterion for selection of the banks in this chapter has been the recommendations of our interviewee panel. In addition, we have incorporated some of the research of banking consultants such as BCG who have also focused on successful business models for the future. Finally, our own research into banking best practice has suggested a few institutions which also fit the parameters established in the earlier chapters.

The banks selected are based in both developed and emerging national markets. Most are essentially retail or commercial banking institutions either with a national focus, significant international operations, or an actual global business model. The sample also includes two who fit the BCG category of global leaders in a specialist activity: investment banking and wealth management.

Many excellent banks have not been included in this listing. For example, it does not include any of the myriad of local or community banks, who in markets like the US have successfully navigated the current banking crisis and who should continue to do so given their core focus on client deposits and loans. But in aggregate the selection is a logical extension of the general precepts for major institutions articulated by our interviewees.

Each case study contains three segments. The first is a brief business profile of the bank, its evolution and ownership, financial performance, key business units and relative profit contribution, and other structural elements. This is followed by an analysis of its strategic development focusing on relative priorities and objectives as well as the impact of the current financial and economic turmoil. The case study concludes with our views on the positive dimensions, challenges in achieving the strategic objectives and possible outcomes of the strategy.

The sample thus includes

- *Banco Santander*, a leading Spanish bank with significant local businesses in the UK, Portugal, Spain and Mexico, whose focus is core retail banking based on a common business platform;
- *Banco Itau*, the leading commercial bank in Brazil, which is now the largest domestically owned bank in Latin America;
- *HSBC*, a truly global bank with operations in over 80 developed and emerging markets;
- *UBS' wealth management business*, which operates globally and has the largest share – 3–4% – of this lucrative activity;
- *Goldman Sachs*, a leading global investment bank with strength in risk management and a remarkable culture which, unlike most of its peers, has survived the banking crisis;
- *Standard Chartered Bank*, a rare example of a Western-owned commercial bank which has built a successful emerging market business in the Asia-Pacific region;
- *JPMorgan Chase*, a strong US bank with global product diversification, which has become a role model for disciplined risk management at the top of the bank;
- *Wells Fargo*, a disciplined US retail bank which has made an opportunistic and transforming acquisition at the height of the crisis to become a national leader.

This list should not be regarded as a 'magic circle' of success stories from the past or for the future, but rather a selection of banks whose generic strategies have attracted the favourable comments of a range of banking peers and experts and which appear to have navigated with some success the 2007–2009 debacle. The core elements of their strategies are aligned with the key success factors and recommendations cited by our experts in the book's earlier chapters.

None has remained untouched by the crisis, and inclusion in this listing is no assurance of continued success. For example, the 'brand' of UBS' wealth management business has suffered from the massive losses in sub-prime exposure of UBS' separately managed investment banking division, while Goldman Sachs reported in 2008 the first quarterly loss of its decade of existence as a public company. Santander and HSBC are among the many banks that have been touched by the Madoff fraud. Yet their core business models are viewed overall as likely to produce superior results in the long term.

Banco Itau: An agreed merger creates Latin America's largest indigenous financial group with a focused strategy

Business profile

Following its agreed merger with rival Unibanco announced in November 2008, the Banco Itau group will become the largest financial institution not only in Brazil but also in Latin America with 11% of the retail financial services sector in its dynamic home market. Its outstanding growth record, financial performance, and focused and conservative strategy are rare among domestic banks in the BRIC countries which are the target of so many Western banks.

A publicly quoted company in which the Setubal family has a significant minority interest, Itau was established in 1945 and has since grown organically as well as by acquisitions, such as the local businesses of Bank Boston and the Austrian Creditanstalt. Earnings per share of the main operating company, Banco Itau Holding Financeira (BIHF), have increased at a compound rate of 27% since 1994, and dollar investors have achieved an annual compound return on their shares of 25% over the past decade. Return on investment for BIHF in 2007 was 27% – the same level as in 2000. Itau is well capitalized with regulatory capital of 15% in 2008. At mid-2008, BIHF's asset base was $216 billion equivalent.

The Egydio de Souza Aranha family, a member of which is the group's CEO, has a minority stake in the quoted holding company Itausa, which in turn owns a controlling 86% of the common shares of BIHF. As discussed below, BIHF owns 100% of the three functional operating units: Itaubanco (retail and SME banking), Itau BBA (corporate and investment banking) and Itaucred (credit cards and vehicle finance). Following the merger, the two groups' holdings will be merged into a company called Itau Unibanco Holding SA.

The macro-economic environment for Brazilian banks has evolved favourably in recent years despite the global crisis which has impacted so many emerging markets. Inflation has been brought down by firm monetary and fiscal policy with the result that real interest rates are actually negative, government debt has declined steadily, bank credit is a relatively modest 36% of GDP, which has expanded at 3–4% in recent years, and net interest margins have stabilized at about 11% of the banks' loan book. Mortgage lending is a modest 2% of GDP and thus offers useful growth potential without the excesses seen in other markets.

Itau's superior financial performance has continued during the dramatic improvement of Brazil's macro-economic environment as well as the recent global banking crisis. Its net interest margin has remained steady at about 11% as interest rates have declined along with inflation, while its cost/income ratio has dropped steadily from 62% in 2001 to 43% in the first half of 2008. Net income has increased in each year except 2006 when loss provisions rose sharply. While management has slowed the group's loan growth rate during the crisis, funding has not been a problem. Loan volumes in key segments rose by 30–35% in the crisis year of 2008, and loss provisions will remain at the 2007 level.

Strategic positioning

Itau is a 'multiple bank' under Brazilian regulations with separate corporate entities providing its broad product range. Its core focus has traditionally been to serve retail and SME clients through Itaubanco, which accounts for 57% of BIHF's operating profits and 75% of its loan portfolio. The group is the dominant provider in Brazil of home mortgages (20%), credit cards (22%) and vehicle finance (26%). It also accounts for 13.9% of the country's branch network, which has been growing strongly in recent years, 15% of the fund management sector and 17% of the insurance market. As indicated above, the merger with Unibanco will augment these market positions.

In 2002, the group acquired the Brazilian interests of the Austrian bank Creditanstalt and created Banco BBA to provide corporate and investment banking services. This was followed by the acquisition in 2006 of the operations in Brazil, Chile and Uruguay of BankBoston from Bank of America. Banco BBA now is the largest wholesale bank in Brazil with 11% of the market. In 2007, the bank led the market in fixed income underwritings and ranked second in M & A transactions and equity operations.

In large part because of the BankBoston acquisition, Itau is the most international of the Brazilian banks. A total of $6.3 billion had been invested by 2008 in the group's international network.

Strategy evaluation

While other major banks in the BRIC category have demonstrated excellent profit growth, Itau stands out among them by its diversity, focused management and conservative risk policies. It would appear to have navigated the current banking crisis successfully, with no reported damage from the sub-prime sector or funding problems.

Its merger with the third largest Brazilian bank, Unibanco, is in many ways a parallel with Wells Fargo's more opportunistic purchase of Wachovia to create a leading banking institution in its home market.

One possible threat to the new Itau is the advent of strong competition from foreign-owned banks such as Santander with an efficient retail network, substantial capital and highly regarded management team. Another is the challenge of sustaining domestic growth outside its home markets in Latin America. Finally, in the view of international investors, Itau will understandably be viewed as a play on Brazil as a market. Several of our interviewees noted that should Brazil's macro-economic and political situation deteriorate, as have those of other former growth markets like the CEE, Itau could become vulnerable in such an international comparison.

Goldman Sachs: One of the remaining independent global investment banks reaffirms its strategy despite the turmoil

Business profile

One of the two major global institutional securities firms remaining independent following the collapse of its peers in late 2008, Goldman Sachs traces its roots to the late nineteenth century as a domestic US commercial paper dealer owned by its partners. Since then, it has built a major international business; survived losses in earlier crises such as the Penn Central failure in 1970 and the Robert Maxwell fraud in the 1990s; become a leader in global M & A, equity underwriting and prime brokerage and converted its partnership into a quoted company in 1999.

Its financial results reflect its focus on high margin businesses and the boom in financial services since then. In 2007, its operating margin was a remarkable 38.3% of revenues. As indicated in Figure 8.1, between 1999 and 2007 its average return on tangible equity was 26%, and its compound annual increase in book value was 19%. Goldman's equity capital at end 2008 was $64 billion. In the final quarter of 2008, however, Goldman reported its first loss since going public, largely from write-downs on its direct investment portfolio rather than sub-prime–related securities.

In late 2008, when most of its US-based rivals were collapsed into universal banks or went bankrupt, only Goldman (and its long-standing rival Morgan Stanley) remained independent, albeit after conversion to banking status under the regulatory regime of

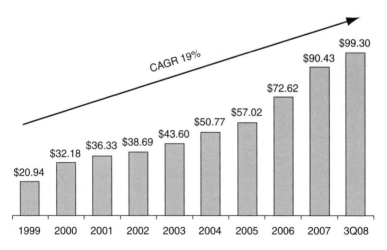

Figure 8.1 Growth in Goldman Sachs' book value per share – 1999 to 3Q08
Source: Goldman Sachs.

the Federal Reserve System. Despite criticism by analysts for excessive leverage, the Fed deemed the firm 'well capitalized' based on Goldman's Tier 1 capital base of 15.6% at end 2008, which had been augmented by government funds and a major equity investment by the noted value investor Warren Buffett.

Despite its sustained expansion in physical terms to a level of about 30,000 employees, Goldman has retained many of the features of its partnership tradition. The management committee and chief executive manage the business in a highly disciplined fashion with extensive collaboration among businesses, rigorous risk controls and client focus as integral dimensions of its culture.

Strategic positioning

Goldman's strategic development has been characterized by agility in moving into attractive lines of business, focus on highly profitable activities, willingness to take risk and use its capital to maximum effect, and an aggressive approach to capitalizing on business opportunities.

It has three major lines of business. *Investment banking*, its traditional focus, includes its global status as a leading M & A advisor and equity underwriter, and accounted for 16% of 2007 revenues. *Asset management and securities services*, also with 16% of the total, comprises its activity as a major asset manager with roughly $800 billion in funds under management as well as its role as one of the two leading prime brokers who service hedge fund and other institutional investors. *Trading and principal investing*, the largest business with 68% of the total includes its FICC activity of trading in currencies, fixed interest, commodities and other markets globally for its own account. In principal investing, which is equivalent in size to a major portion of the firm's capital, Goldman co-invests with its major individual and institutional clients in so-called merchant banking funds, which totalled $23 billion at the end of 2007.

Overall, roughly 50% of Goldman's revenues are fee-based, with another 32% in FICC trading and 5% in principal investments.

In geographic terms, Goldman has built organically since the 1980s a major global investment banking business. Earnings from the US now account for about half of the total, with Europe 29% and Asia representing 17% and growing rapidly. During the past two years, the firm has invested heavily in the four BRIC markets by obtaining licenses and populating the local units with experienced Goldman professionals.

A central element of Goldman's strategic positioning is its unique culture of internal collaboration and decision making, deliberate but controlled risk-taking, tradition of support for clients, and willingness to make difficult decisions. Thus the firm has traditionally maintained the total remuneration of its professionals and staff below the industry standard of 50% of revenues. Former Goldman professionals now play a major role in the senior management of other financial institutions, corporate organizations and governmental bodies, and the firm encourages many of its managing directors to leave in mid career for other positions where they might collaborate with the firm in various roles.

As a result of the banking crisis, Goldman has significantly reduced its leverage ratio (from 245% to 82% of tangible equity), which has received the imprimatur of the Federal Reserve authorities, and continued to mark its assets to market, unlike many other institutions. While it is understood that the firm's CEO contacted his counterpart at Citigroup at the depth of the banking crisis in October 2008, it is believed that no substantive discussions took place over a possible linkage.

Strategic evaluation

Goldman Sachs is a useful case study not only because of its role as a leading investment bank but also as an example of a focused, disciplined financial institution able to survive in difficult times in a specific global speciality. Several of our interviewees believe that the bank's model is 'broken' in the sense that its risk appetite is not realistic for a quoted company in an environment of de-leveraging and de-risking.

This is possible, but management has been clear about its intention to sustain its historical strategy and ability over the cycle to achieve its long-standing 20% ROTE goal – despite reducing leverage and becoming subject to Federal Reserve guidelines. It is not at all certain that many such investment banks will survive the current crisis as independent entities, but should Goldman do so it will reap the benefits of its substantial holdings in co-investments and ability to profit from market opportunities in the eventual recovery. Its current and former management are still significant stockholders in the company and are likely to guide the firm to maximize its returns in the difficult market it faces.

Management speaks of the opportunities 'to provide optionality in a dislocated market' such as the firm now faces as being those which it traditionally has exploited with great success. Over its long history Goldman has repeatedly re-invented itself, in particular after a crisis period, on the back of its innovative and disciplined professional team. Many of its core businesses, such as investment banking and prime brokerage, will be depressed for some time as a result of the financial and economic crisis.

Brad Hintz, an experienced equity analyst and former investment banker himself, summarizes the situation nicely in a quotation in the *Financial Times*:

> Goldman Sachs is still going to be an amazing firm. It's just going to have to change!

Over the past few decades, Goldman has morphed from a classic investment bank earning fees from intermediation and providing advice to one heavily reliant on using its capital to take risk positions. Market rumours at the time of writing call for the next step to be a newly minted commercial bank to acquire a deposit-taking or cash management franchise.

HSBC: The world's largest bank focuses on growth markets with interconnectivity to developed ones

Business profile

With $128 billion in Tier 1 capital in mid-2008, HSBC is a truly global bank with operations in over 80 countries, some 315,000 employees and 10,000 offices around the globe. Leveraging its well-known brand of 'the world's local bank', management aims to increase its profit contribution from growth, or emerging, markets from its present 40% to 60% of the total in the medium term.

While suffering somewhat from the 2007–2008 banking crisis, HSBC's earning power reflects its diversity and strength in dynamic market segments. Its current investor guidance calls for a target ROE of between 15% and 19% over the economic cycle. In the first half of 2008, despite an actual loss in North America due to sub-prime loans and investment banking write-downs, group ROE was an impressive 15.4%. The group's Tier 1 ratio in mid-2008 was a relatively high 8.8%.

Since its formation in 1865 as a trade finance specialist in Hong Kong, the group has grown in large part by strategic acquisitions. In the 1980s and 1990s, following organic growth in the Asia-Pacific region, major acquisitions in the US (the retail bank Marine Midland) and the UK (Midland Bank) reflected a strategy of diversifying away from reliance on this region. Leading banks in Latin America (Bital in Mexico, Bamerindus in Brazil and Banco Roberts in Argentina) as well as Europe (CCF in France, Trinkhaus in Germany and several private banks in Switzerland) have been acquired to create a truly global network.

Of the 50 acquisitions during the period 1999–2006 examined in a survey by Deutsche Bank, however, the purchase of a sub-prime lender in 2003 in the US, Household Finance, has since generated losses which reduced the overall annual gain from acquisitions during that period to a modest 6.6% per annum. Losses from sub-prime continue to weigh upon the group's P & L.

Strategic positioning

HSBC's strategy has focused on building a customer deposit base to ensure group liquidity as well as diversifying in all three strategic dimensions (client, product and geography). In recent years, three guidelines have underpinned the strategy: emerging markets will grow faster than developed ones, world trade will expand faster than world output and people will live longer. As indicated above, earnings from emerging markets are targeted to increase from the current 40% to 60% of the total.

To focus this large and diverse organization more sharply, in 2007 management gave priority to initiatives which would both focus on emerging markets as well as provide 'connectivity' between these markets and existing developed ones. 'Joining up' the various entities will be a major objective to increase revenues, employee engagement and benefit from scale. The implication is that some divestitures which do not meet these criteria will be made. Thus the group sold in 2008 its French retail network acquired with CCF.

In organizational terms, the group is managed globally around four major client segments:

- *Personal financial services* (PFS), or retail banking, has roughly 120 million clients. Impacted negatively in 2007–2008 by sub-prime losses in the US, it accounted for only 23% of pre-tax profits in the first half of 2008, down from 43% in 2006.
- *Commercial banking* (CB) for roughly 4500 small and mid-sized companies has been a source of steadily growing profit and high margins, especially in developing markets. During the first half of 2008, it accounted for an impressive 44% of the pre-tax total.
- *Global banking and markets* (GBM) serves some 4000 major corporate and institutional relationships with credit, money transmission, investment banking and other services. Depressed by write-downs linked to the banking crisis, its contribution to pre-tax in the first half of 2008 was 26% of the total; down slightly from 27% in 2006.
- *Private banking* (PB), the smallest unit with 8% of total pre-tax in the first half of 2008, manages about $500 billion in customer funds, largely from a base in Switzerland.

In geographic terms, recent pre-tax performance has been marked by the collapse of income from North America, due largely to sub-prime losses, from $4.7 billion, or 21% of the global total, to an actual loss of $2.9 billion during the first half of 2008. Europe, on the other hand, has sustained its performance and in the first half of 2008 accounted for an impressive 50% of the global total with major contributions from each client segment. Hong Kong and the balance of Asia-Pacific together continue to represent the largest overall contribution with 55% of 2007 pre-tax and 67% in the first half of 2008.

Strategic evaluation

HSBC's global scope and size drives both its strategic strengths and weaknesses.

On the one hand, its size, diversity, massive liquidity and capital strength have made the group a net winner from the banking crisis. In the UK, for example, one of our interviewees noted that the bank could have scooped up the remaining large UK banks at a modest cost had it not have been for the obvious need for competitive balance.

And its size has enabled it to cope with the massive losses from its sub-prime exposure in the US domestic market and still retain its pristine credit rating.

On the other hand, its size and complexity inevitably mean a slower decision-making process and less entrepreneurial initiative. Ironically, the 2003 acquisition of Household Finance was hailed for years as an entrepreneurial success: a major bank taking a view on an emerging growth sector, which sadly ended in disastrous losses. Interestingly enough, HSBC's chief financial officer Doug Flint, interviewed in 2004 for another book by the author, noted prophetically in commenting on the importance of liquidity in a crisis:

> The nightmare scenario is that something unexpected happens; liquidity falls away, and there's a spiral of failures. People take liquidity for granted. And with a fragmented regulatory system, you have people trying to find ways to take the maximum risk for the minimum of capital.

It would have required a unique crystal ball to predict that the HFC acquisition in the previous year would arguably play a role in triggering that nightmare scenario. But HSBC proved its ability to deal with the liquidity crisis which followed.

Another potential weakness of the strategy is being spread too thin to take advantage of individual opportunities. Several of our interviewees prefer the more focused strategy of a bank like Santander which aims for deep penetration of a limited number of attractive markets. Thus while China is an obvious priority for HSBC and the group has over 80 outlets in the country plus a number of minority interests in domestic financial institutions, the overall weight of China in the group's earnings is probably relatively low compared to its economic potential.

On balance, however, HSBC has demonstrated the virtues of size and scope. Should it be able to achieve over the cycle its target of 15–19% ROE, this would place it well above the likely results forecast for the banking sector over the intermediate term by our interviewees. Compared to other massive global banks such as Citibank, its management appears to have prioritized and controlled its strategic development to maximize shareholder value.

JPMorgan Chase: Disciplined risk management and diversified business base sustain the business model during the turmoil

Business profile

The product of a transforming 2004 merger which united the US regional bank BancOne and the diversified JPMorgan Chase under the latter's brand, the group boasts impressive franchises in its six business units.

Despite massive write-downs which produced a loss in its investment banking unit in 2008 as well as problems in its US consumer banking business, the bank remained in the black for the year with a modest 4% ROE, down from 13% in 2007.

In addition, at the height of the crisis JPMorgan Chase was able to acquire with government support two failed institutions, the US mortgage bank WaMu and the investment bank Bear Stearns. At year-end 2008 the company had an impressive Tier 1 capital of 10.8%. Under the leadership of CEO Jamie Dimon from the former BancOne who took over the top job in 2006, JPMorgan Chase has become a role model for successful top-down risk management.

Today one of the three largest banking institutions in the US, JPMorgan Chase is the product of a series of mergers in the US which began in the early 1990s. The former Chemical Bank acquired another commercial bank, Manufacturers Hanover in 1991, followed by the Chase Manhattan Bank in 1996. The investment bank JPMorgan was then acquired in 2000.

Strategic positioning

The group's business model since the formative 2004 merger has been based on its six lines of business summarized in Figure 8.2, which represents the breakdown in profit contribution for the year 2008 partially offset by the loss incurred in the investment banking business.

In its 17-state franchise in the Northeastern US, JPMorgan Chase has a major market position with over 3000 retail branches, as well as major specialist credit card, auto finance and mortgage units. In commercial banking in this region, the bank boasts a leading 14% market share. Its investment banking business ranks among the top three global players in virtually all major segments, with particular

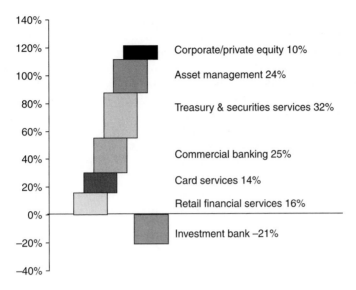

Figure 8.2 Profile of JPMorgan Chase net income contribution by line of business for 2008
Source: DIBC analysis of JPMorgan Chase financials.

strength in fixed income and credit products. Building on the original JPMorgan asset management franchise, the group managed $1.1 trillion of third party funds at year-end 2007 and is the largest manager of hedge funds.

While several of its business units are currently under pressure from the credit crisis, others are quite profitable. For the final quarter of 2008, its commercial (SME) unit boasted an ROE of 24%, its treasury and securities services business earned one of 47%, while the asset management group yielded an ROE of 14%.

From the merger in 2004 with the BancOne regional bank, the group acquired its current chief executive, Jamie Dimon, who had been responsible for BancOne's previous turnaround. On assuming executive responsibility for the merged group, Dimon has extended the reputation for successful integration established by his predecessors.

Our interview series confirmed Dimon's reputation for a strong, risk-oriented, top-down leadership which is widely believed to have accounted for its relative success in navigating the problems thrown up by the banking crisis.

One of Dimon's senior colleagues noted in our interview that

> He has clear ideas of what is important and is committed to executing these ideas. He has three big ideas: a core competence in IT, in particular for risk management; a fortress balance sheet, and a single minded focus on costs. Managing size and complexity is all about people. It's easy to say 'we have good risk management.' But you can't delegate it: the CEO is the chief risk manager.

Another senior commercial banking executive in the group whose career antedated the arrival of Dimon notes that

> There's more clarity about who's in charge. Dimon is forceful, very hands on, with a team who's worked with him for years. He's a 'non-bank' CEO with a clear focus on the bottom line. He sets the parameters; if you meet them, he let's you run the business. He believes banking is not unique! He has a distinct passion for infrastructure with a deep understanding of how a bank works; he has a CFO background.

One of Dimon's early decisions was to scrap the comprehensive outsourcing agreement of the bank with IBM – the largest such deal in history. He has been quoted as saying before he took over the bank's management: 'you didn't know what you were doing' in signing up with IBM.

The consensus of interviewees for this report was that JPMorgan Chase under his leadership is the best example of M & A success in the US in recent years. Typical comments included:

> 'success in large, complex banks requires hands-on senior management – especially in risk management – like Jamie Dimon's'
> 'Jamie has pulled it off – no big mistakes'
> 'the best US case study. He executed exactly as planned and met promises to stockholders and regulators. There's a clear definition of who's in charge'
> 'He created a model of integration of banks with different cultures and systems. There's a strong culture of team development. He's

no cream puff – very analytical – and engenders respect and loyalty. He's taken the merged bank to a new level for a universal bank – it's what allows JPMorgan to manage complexity better than others'.

Strategic evaluation

In only a few years, Dimon has integrated a number of under-performing businesses, driven costs down, installed effective risk management processes and created a common culture for the group. In the context of the current credit crisis which has brought down a number of peer institutions, JPMorgan stands out as a remarkable success study despite its losses in 2007–2008.

Perhaps most impressive of all is the team approach; our interviewees confirm that management is not a one man band. While reputations of chief executives can be extremely fragile, especially in the ferociously competitive investment banking world, that of Dimon would appear to be quite solidly based.

With its broadly based business profile and strong balance sheet, the group is well positioned for the future. Having acquired, with US government support, two major problem institutions – Bear Stearns and WaMu – in 2008 during the crisis, JPMorgan Chase has integrated them onto its existing platforms and should reap significant profits over the longer term from its low cost of acquisition. Its diversification should stand it in good stead as banks traverse the difficult period of replacing the businesses discredited by the crisis and dealing with less buoyant growth prospects.

A senior JPMorgan Chase banker interviewed for this profile summarized management's business strategy going forward:

> There's no change in the model. We'll retain the six lines of business. Size is not an issue if the bank is well managed. Apart from serving its clients, our strategy will focus on two objectives: managing risk and protecting margins, which will be crucial for everybody. The implication is that growth will be primarily by acquisition of distressed firms; growth in core businesses like mortgages and credit cards will be tied to the economy and driven by the macro environment. We won't sell businesses like asset management. We've got the capacity to integrate both Bear Stearns

and WaMu on our existing platforms. The group will grow because we're well capitalized and can take advantage of opportunities and avoid risk.

Santander group: A successful model of disciplined focus, geographic diversity and a proven retail banking capability

Business profile

Created from successive mergers by the original Banco Santander with several leading Spanish banks beginning in the 1990s, the Santander Group is now the largest Spanish banking group with major retail franchises also in Portugal, the UK, Brazil, Chile and Mexico.

With an equity base at the end of the third quarter of 2008 of €51 billion, Santander is the fourth largest bank in Europe and one of the 20 largest banks in the world. It has the largest branch network – some 14,000 units – of any bank in the world. Its ROE in 2007 of 23.2% compares favourably with an average of its European peers of 16.8%, largely due to its strength in high margin Latin American retail markets. In addition, it benefits from a much lower cost/income ratio of 47.3% against the peers' 59.5%, which is in part attributable to its tested Partenon global retail banking platform.

Earnings growth has been both balanced and steady even during the current crisis period. While third quarter 2008 earnings slipped from the prior year level due to higher loss provisions, all major units reported earnings growth for the first nine months of the year. Attributable earnings per share for the period rose 8% for the period, in sharp contrast to declines for most leading banks.

A key driver of its impressive earnings growth is success in not only making profitable acquisitions but also in divesting businesses at a profit. A well-advertised example of this success is Santander's participation in the RBS-led syndicate which acquired ABN AMRO in 2007. While other members of the syndicate have had serious problems with their share of the deal, Santander not only acquired its desired crown jewel, Banco Real, which doubled its base in the lucrative Brazilian market, but also enabled Santander to on-sell an

Italian bank, Interbanca, to another Italian institution at a price which reduced its total cost for the deal by half.

The group's core equity ratio of 6.3% at September 2008 was somewhat above management's 6.0% target. The direct impact of the banking crisis on Santander has been limited, with little exposure to toxic structured products. Loss provisions were increased in 2008 by 67%, however, reflecting possible losses in the Brazilian market.

Strategic positioning

In geographic terms, Santander has diversified successfully outside its home Spanish market, largely by acquisitions in the UK and Latin America. Figure 8.3 provides the relative importance in risk-weighted assets for the first nine months of 2008 by region. There are three core management entities based on geographic region: Continental Europe with roughly half of the total profit, the UK with 13% and Latin America with 39% (including Banco Real). Santander has a 13%

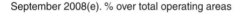

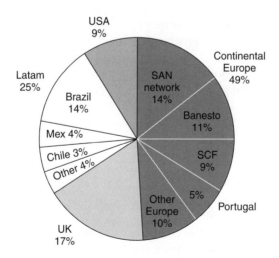

Figure 8.3 Santander's risk-weighted assets by geographical area – September 2008
Source: Grupo Santander.

market share in Spain, with roughly 10% in Brazil, 15% in Mexico and 21% in Chile. In the UK it is now the third largest deposit taker following the acquisition of two smaller banks to complement its earlier purchase of Abbey National.

Outside this market area, Santander has long contemplated building a presence in the US, and in 2007–2008 it bought control of Sovereign Bank, a regional bank which has suffered from the real estate crisis.

The group's product focus globally is essentially the retail/SME segment with particular strength in consumer finance, in which it is now active in 20 different markets. In the first quarter of 2008, retail earnings accounted for 77% of the group's pre-tax result, with the balance from Global Wholesale Banking and Asset Management. Its retail strategy is built around the global use of its Partenon retail banking system, which was developed in its Banesto subsidiary and is being introduced throughout its network. While it must be modified to meet local requirements, Partenon provides the customer profile information so often missing in other banks' legacy systems as well as significantly reducing the group's cost base. The increase in absolute costs for the group has declined in each quarter since the third period of 2007, thus creating an even stronger 'jaws' impact to match its above-par revenue growth.

The advent of the banking crisis has produced a new 'back to basics' business model, whose main elements are summarized in Figure 8.4, all of which have been present in the past but which now will be highlighted. More specifically, management is focused on two challenges: addressing the slowdown in key performance metrics, and integrating the new acquisitions, along with the Partenon installation.

Strategic evaluation

Santander's strategy of focus on mass market retail, diversity of geographic presence and opportunistic acquisitions has paid off. The bank is one of those most cited in answer to our question of 'whose strategic model has been the most successful?' One of the few major banks in developed markets to report actual earnings growth for the crisis year of 2008, Santander management plans no major changes to its strategic model. As indicated in our interview with Matias Inciarte

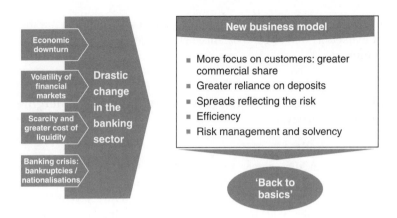

Figure 8.4 Santander's response to the banking crisis
Source: Grupo Santander.

(Chapter 5), geographic diversity will remain a hallmark of its development. At the same time, divestitures outside the core retail banking segment take place; Santander's asset management business has been put up for sale in 2008.

What threats might the group face in the future? Its home market of Spain is passing through a major real estate-driven crisis, although like its peers the bank has created substantial loss reserves. The UK is also facing a continued real estate downturn which might impact Abbey's growth prospects. Brazil has been a key source of growth, and Santander is vulnerable to volatility in this important market. As for expansion in the US, our interview indicated that further expansion of the Sovereign business is likely to await resolution of problems in the home market.

Finally, there is a risk that management's opportunistic acquisition strategy could result in overpaying for a target company. Thus the minority interest in Sovereign in the US in retrospect looked expensive, although the purchase of the balance brought the average cost considerably lower.

On balance, however, the Santander business model is likely to continue to produce superior earnings growth. Discipline in client focus – and willingness to invest in the systems needed to service profitably the key retail market – is a hallmark of this model. And in geographic terms, there has been both focus on a limited number of markets as well as good balance between developed and emerging countries.

Standard Chartered Bank: A successful pure play emerging market strategy

Business profile

Created from the merger in 1969 of two London-based international banks, Standard Chartered Bank has focused geographically on emerging markets in Asia, the Middle East and Africa. While larger global banks like HSBC have also prioritized these markets, StanChart is unique in not having a home country retail market or a major presence in the developed world, and its strategy is thus of particular interest as a role model.

It is regulated in the UK by the Financial Services Authority (FSA) despite having only headquarters and central operating units in the country. While having been determined to be 'systemically important' to the UK banking system in late 2008, the bank declined to accept any government financial support. Our interview for this case study indicated that the global reputation of the FSA as a respected regulator has been a critical success factor in its penetration of target emerging markets.

With an equity base at mid-2008 of $21 billion, the group is a mid-sized institution but still operates in over 70 countries with about 1750 branches and 75,000 in staff. A number of acquisitions in Asia have supplemented organic growth. In 2005, Korea First Bank, the nation's seventh largest, was acquired, while United Bank of Pakistan (with 7% of that market) and Hsinchu in Taiwan were purchased in 2006 as well as investment in a joint venture in Indonesia. Most recently, StanChart acquired American Express, a smaller international bank with strength in private banking and cash management.

In the first half of 2008, an impressive return on operating equity of 25% was achieved, and earnings growth for the half year was 31%. Net interest margins and the cost/income ratio have been stable, with fee income contributing significant growth. In mid-2008, the bank's Tier 1 ratio was 8.5%, near the top of management's target range. StanChart is largely self-funding, with an impressive 85% loan/deposit ratio.

Strategic positioning

The bank's strategy is summed up in the phrase 'to be the best international bank, leading the way in Asia, Africa and the Middle East'. This strategy, however, dates back only several years under the present management team. Previous management strategies were marked by unsuccessful efforts to build durable businesses in a wide range of developed as well as emerging markets.

In executing its current strategy, management has become aware of the difficulty in building a core retail business beyond an initial 3–4% penetration which can be achieved in a targeted marketing programme based on the mortgage product. In its 'home' markets of Singapore and Hong Kong in which it has been present for decades, StanChart for some time was essentially a provider of a limited range of retail products. Heavy investment in the product range has since enabled the bank to achieve the status of a relationship bank equipped with a full range of retail products to reap the scale benefits from cross selling.

This is not valid for the massive target markets of India and China, where a more selective approach is needed to build market share. Thus, while the bank has been active in India for some 150 years, market share is still modest with branches being opened one by one, and India has become a significant contributor to global profits. This approach is even more relevant for China, where the entry of foreign banks like StanChart has been quite recent as well as restricted to certain cities, and few foreign banks are yet making significant profits. On the other hand, such new branches move into the black generally after 18 months of operations.

Finally, while acquisitions in the target markets have brought useful market share gains with them, we understand that integration has posed some challenges as management has focused on building a client-centred business.

Within the global brief of focus on emerging markets, the priority countries are India and China, which to date have been penetrated by organic expansion. In India, which became the second largest national profit source in the first half of 2008 with 23% of pre-tax profits, StanChart in 2006 had a total of 81 branches with 14,000 employees. While the bank aims at being a leading foreign bank in China as that market opens up, the country does not figure among the major national sources of profit. Hong Kong remains the largest contributor with 25% of June 2008 pre-tax profits, followed in third place by Singapore with 12%.

The group's product range is highly diversified, especially for a bank of its size. Figure 8.5 provides data setting out both its geographic scope and product breakdown as a percentage of pre-tax operating profit. Whereas in 2006 there was a rough balance between the core retail and wholesale businesses, by mid-2008 the latter had surged to 67% of operating profit reflecting the investment costs of building a branch network and product capability.

In revenue terms, the global markets function provided the largest single contribution with 32%, followed by wealth management and deposit gathering with 22%.

Rather than set specific financial targets for its businesses, the bank relies more on broader strategic goals. Thus in wholesale banking,

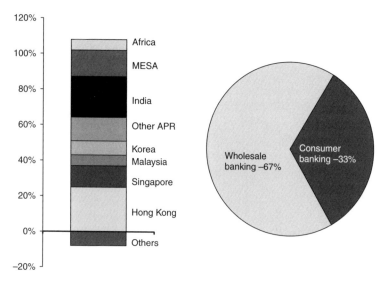

Figure 8.5   Breakdown of Standard Chartered's pre-tax profit by geography and function – first half 2008

Source: Standard Chartered data, DIBC analysis.

the goal is to become a preferred provider to target clients in seven national markets. In retail/commercial banking, it is to become one of the top three providers in target markets as the 'best international bank'. A relationship-driven, client-focused culture is seen as a critical success factor. Having learned from earlier experience with sub-scale shares in a wide range of markets, StanChart management now focuses only on a limited range of target markets it knows well.

A recent strategic priority has been to build a private banking/wealth management business, in large part on the back of the American Express client base. With an estimated third of the world's millionaires living in its market area, wealth management is a logical growth target. To recoup its late start in the business, Standard Chartered opened a remarkable 11 offices in May–June 2007, and the bank now has private banking offices in 16 countries. To minimize the conflict with other units which 'own' these clients, private banking revenues and costs are included within the retail bank.

Strategic evaluation

While it can trace its origins to offices in Shanghai and Calcutta opened by its predecessor banks in 1853 – before even HSBC opened its doors in the region – Standard Chartered's management has only in recent years focused on building its presence in the growth markets of Asia-Pacific and the Middle East. At the same time, it is a medium-sized institution with activities across the product spectrum and competes with global giants such as Citibank and HSBC as well as a plethora of local rivals.

Despite these constraints, the group has an excellent record of profitable growth and has suffered no major losses from the current crisis. With a premium rating driven by its focus on key emerging markets, Standard Chartered should be able to grow by acquisition and organically in its target markets. Over time, however, there may well be a need to focus scarce resources on national markets such as India where it is capable of creating critical mass. Another alternative is a major merger or acquisition designed to accelerate penetration in its target markets.

In this context, the bank has learned from experience that heavy investment in products and facilities is necessary to build the preferred relationship and client focus necessary to achieve its strategic goals.

UBS: A unique global wealth management business could stand alone as a strategic role model

Business profile of the group

Formed in 1998 by the merger of Swiss Bank Corporation and Union Bank of Switzerland, UBS is Switzerland's largest banking institution. Since the merger, the group has built its strategy around three businesses: wealth management, where it is the global leader, asset management and investment banking.

While the first two businesses have performed well in recent years, in 2007–2008 the group's investment banking business, in particular its fixed income activity which became heavily involved in the US sub-prime problems, has undermined both its capital position and image as a professional risk manager. With over $40 billion in write-offs during this period, UBS has suffered the most of any European institution during the current credit crisis. A massive CHF 15 billion loss in the investment banking arm plunged UBS into a group deficit in 2007, the group's first since its formation, and which widened in the first half of 2008. A new management team installed in late 2007 has focused on rebuilding the capital position, improving risk management processes and determining the fate of the damaged investment banking activity.

UBS has also suffered damage to its reputation during the past year when a US court charged the bank with illegally managing the accounts of US citizens who had been using the bank to avoid US tax. As a result, UBS has closed down its US offshore banking business.

Long renowned for its capital strength and superior earning power, in 2006 UBS boasted a Tier 1 ratio of 11.9% and operating return on equity of 24%. Losses in 2007 and the first half of 2008 were roughly offset by new capital, with the Tier 1 ratio edging down to 11.6% in mid-2008.

In organizational terms, by far the most important function is Global Wealth Management and Business Banking Switzerland (GWMBB), which is the subject of this case study.

GWMBB in turn groups three business units: Wealth Management International and Switzerland (WMIS); Wealth Management USA, which includes the retail brokerage activity originally built on Paine Webber acquired in 2000 and Business Banking Switzerland, which encompasses the domestic Swiss retail and corporate banking businesses and operates a network of over 300 branches with individual product market shares in excess of 20%. In aggregate, UBS' customer funds under management from these three units totalled CHF 1.9 trillion at September 2008, which places it first globally with an estimated 3–4% of the world's fragmented wealth management market. Roughly, two-thirds of GWMBB's profits are derived from the WMIS unit.

In terms of total earnings contribution, operating earnings from GWMBB dominated UBS' group profits in 2007 with CHF 9.5 billion, followed by CHF 1.3 billion from Global Asset Management (GAM), an asset manager with about CHF 1 billion in customer funds and operations in 23 countries. With regard to the loss-making investment banking business, the new management team is actively seeking to revamp its problem fixed income activity and is considering a number of options to restore profitability.

The following analysis sets forth the argument that UBS' wealth management business is a unique case study of a global business which could stand on its own as one of the rare examples of a highly successful 'narrow banking' activity on a global scale. We do not argue that this is the appropriate outcome – as discussed below, management has presumably decided against it – but that it demonstrates how a successful narrow activity can stand alone in a highly competitive marketplace.

Wealth management strategic positioning

The wealth management activity incorporated in GWMBB, as indicated above, is the world's largest. The comprehensive product range includes investment and portfolio management, financial planning, wealth management and corporate financial advisory services. UBS offers tailor-made products to a full range of clients from affluent to 'key clients' with over CHF 50 billion in assets. In 2001, a European Wealth Management initiative was launched to build a stronger onshore presence in major European markets, with the number of client advisors rising from 177 to 870 by 2007.

Figure 8.6 indicates management's views of the likely growth rate of individual markets and the relative profitability for UBS in each.

In the US market, the separately managed Wealth Management USA unit has an estimated market share of 16% with over 8000

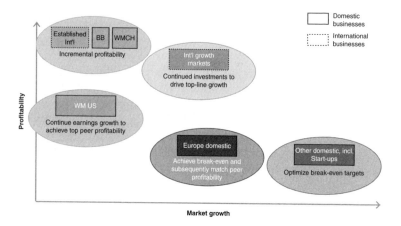

Figure 8.6 UBS's wealth management positioning by national market
Source: UBS.

financial advisors operating through around 440 offices which target affluent and HNW/UHNW clients.

UBS' wealth management strategy is characterized by globality, strong management processes, an active approach to acquisitions and a willingness to invest heavily in systems and human resources.

With total wealth management staff of over 51,000 and more than 90 operating locations around the world, UBS is the most global of its peers. In 2006, Europe accounted for 55% of total assets under management, with the Americas 18%, Asia-Pacific 16% and the Middle East 11%. The group's progress in penetrating the dynamic Asia-Pacific market is particularly impressive.

Globality is also present in UBS' segmentation strategy, which has two dimensions: complexity of service model and affinity. There are four basic levels of complexity based on client funds under management: savers (the affluent market); those with up to roughly $5 million, who are offered funds or 'menus' for their portfolios; clients with up to $50 million, who receive a detailed, tailor-made service; and those over $50 million who are effectively managed as an institution with the equivalent of a family office status. In addition, the factor of affinity plays a role. For those major segments with a common background, such as entrepreneurs, specialized teams help to use a common 'language' to meet the specific needs of that segment. Products are designed for each client segment.

Acquisitions have played a major role in creating this global business. In 2000, UBS acquired the major US brokerage firm Paine Webber, followed by several add-on purchases in the US. Separately managed as Wealth Management USA, management has focused on improving profitability by increasing the ratio of discretionary and recurring revenues, moving into higher wealth segments, selling higher margin products and improving the productivity of its advisors. Reflecting the different nature of the US market, the unit's clients are less wealthy and profitable than in WMIS. In the 12 months to September 2008, Wealth Management USA gross margin was 83 basis points, against 111 basis points for WMIS' international business. This profit performance has lagged US peers such as Merrill Lynch and Smith Barney, but progress in improving profitability has been steady.

Over the decade to 2006, UBS made 12 such acquisitions in Europe alone, including a number of purchases from other financial institutions. While there has been some loss of advisors from the acquired firms, management has made significant efforts to align the interests of its acquisitions in terms of values and business strategy.

Investing in processes, people and systems has been a key driver of UBS' outstanding performance in steadily reducing its wealth management cost/income ratio. In each of the years from 2002 to 2007, WMIS has reduced this ratio from above 60% to 51%, while continuing to increase volumes and profits. Net new money per relationship manager doubled between a base period of 2000–2002 and 2006. The compensation model has been adjusted to reward net new business as well as assets under management, while attrition of the relationship manager team has remained well below 10% per annum despite the fierce competition from rivals looking to recruit experienced staff. With trained relationship management staff a key constraint on growth, UBS runs wealth management training universities in Switzerland and Singapore as well as focusing on propagation of best practice and coaching of staff. Its global network is built on a well-tested model ranging from light or 'beachhead' units to fully fledged, or 'leadership', operations depending on the market.

The outcome of this vigorous expansion has been impressive in terms of revenues as well as net profits. In 2007, GWMBB earnings rose 16% to CHF 9.5 billion, while the critical figure of net new money jumped over 30% to CHF 156 million. Over the past year, however, there has been a modest but steady decline in these metrics. Despite the competitive pressure on pricing, margins have been sustained by efforts to increase the proportion of discretionary management and the use of higher margin, alternative products.

Strategic evaluation – wealth management as a standalone business

UBS has created a pacesetter for the global wealth management industry in terms of achieving scale, investing in IT systems and professional development, strength in all major client segments, and true globality with a major presence in the key market areas of the US, Europe and Asia-Pacific. Its US business has not yet reached the performance standards set by its US peers, but the necessary steps have been taken to bridge that gap. Strategic goals for 2010 include building strength in the UHNW segment in the US, embedding onshore businesses in Europe, and exploiting its investment in Asia-Pacific.

As an industry leader, UBS is the obvious target for a wide range of competitors, whether in terms of recruiting its experienced relationship managers or competing for customers. A flood of newcomers to the sector, in particular retail banks who see the potential for sustained earnings growth in wealth management, will understandably target UBS as well as other established leaders, but management believes that existing global players as well as dedicated private, or proximity, banks will offer the most serious competition.

In this context, reputational risk is clearly the greatest threat, at least in the short and medium term. The massive losses in UBS' fixed income business not only have undermined the group's capital base but also its reputation for sound judgements and risk management. In early 2008, net fund outflows for the first time in years replaced the steady gain in net new money of recent years as some clients questioned whether UBS was a safe home for their portfolios. As the group's new chief executive has acknowledged, this issue will be a major preoccupation for the next few years, albeit not life threatening. Whatever the merits of the case, one can assume that competitors are seizing on UBS' losses as a sufficient reason to persuade clients to avoid the bank.

This reputational blow has been reinforced by action taken by the US authorities in connection with enforcing US tax regulations for US taxpayers, an action with which the bank is now collaborating. This embarrassing publicity will continue in the near term to feature in the financial press and hamper the bank's efforts to deal with its overall reputational issue.

What are the arguments for and against setting up UBS' wealth management business on its own? These have presumably been thoroughly debated by the bank's management, but it might be useful to summarize what they might have been. The original synergistic argument for combining the investment banking and wealth management businesses is the potential of cross selling the former's products to the latter's clients. Our interviewees from the Swiss and other banks in our sample believe that the results of such synergies are mixed: investment bankers may have taken advantage of a captive clientele, relied too heavily on this client base, and sold products which were not fit for purpose. And whatever the facts of the case, as indicated above, the reputational damage from the investment banking business for wealth management has been serious. A stronger case can be made for ownership of the asset management product, as our interviewees agreed that a major wealth manager like UBS must have some in-house product manufacture.

And the valuation argument adds to the case against common ownership. With investment banks facing a bleak future in the next few years, the price/earnings argument in favour of wealth management can be compelling.

Whatever the merits of the case and ultimate outcome in terms of corporate structure, our view is that UBS' wealth management business is a case study of the virtues of a highly successful global narrow strategy in financial services.

Wells Fargo: A major US retail bank 'sticks to its knitting' and wins an opportunistic acquisition to create a nationwide institution

Business profile

Known for its disciplined retail-driven business strategy, in late 2008 Wells Fargo profited from the US banking meltdown by winning a contested bid for a US peer, Wachovia Bank which had become a victim of the crisis.

In the US, the merged bank will rank second in deposits, third in loans, fourth in bank-sponsored mutual funds, third in full service brokerage and fifth globally in insurance brokerage. It has an uninterrupted annual growth in income before loss provisions since its formative merger in 1998. In 2008, provisions for losses in home equity and other loans reduced net income sharply, but in comparison with its peers the bank is widely viewed as having suffered less than any of its major peers despite being one of the leading mortgage providers in the US.

Wells' financial record is characterized by consistent growth and relatively high returns. Profits pre-provisions and tax have expanded by 15% annually over the past 10 years and by 25% in the crisis year of 2008. Its ROE over the past 5 years has averaged 18% with one of 15% for the 9 months of the difficult year 2008. The Wachovia acquisition drove Wells' Tier 1 ratio below its long-term target of 8%, but this gap should be filled by incremental earnings over the next few years, and rating agencies have generally welcomed the transaction.

Created in 1989 with the transforming and difficult merger of two major US regionals based in Minneapolis and San Francisco with totally different cultures, Wells, under the leadership of its current Chairman, Richard Kovacevich, has grown organically and through over 280 acquisitions of smaller banks to achieve virtual almost nationwide retail coverage with the purchase of Wachovia, as indicated in Figure 8.7. Until late 2008, Kovacevich was outspoken in his public determination to avoid major acquisitions on the basis that such deals were risky and that Wells could achieve its goals organically.

In October 2008, however, when Wachovia was sinking beneath the weight of problem loans and was offered to Citigroup with government support, Wells made an unsolicited bid which was much more attractive both to stockholders and the government and won the day.

The projected impact of the Wachovia acquisition would appear to justify Wells' reversal of its stance on mergers. The two banks are roughly equal in size of retail network with 11 million retail clients and over 3 million branches each, but Wells is far superior in such

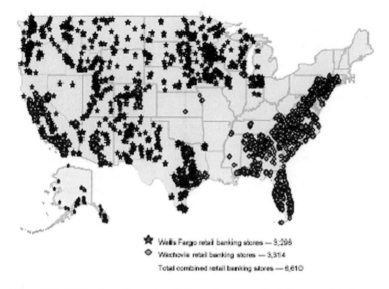

Figure 8.7 Wells Fargo's national branch network following Wachovia acquisition
Source: Courtesy of Wells Fargo.

metrics as credit card penetration, online customers, sales of insurance products and mortgage origination. As indicated below, Wells is the leader in cross selling in the US and would expect to achieve significant gains from the merger in this critical metric. Even after writing off an estimated $60 billion in toxic Wachovia assets, Wells estimates an internal rate of return of 20% on the transaction.

Strategic positioning

Since its formation by merger in 1989, Wells has sustained its vision of being 'the premier provider of financial services in all of our markets'. The focus is thus on selling a wide range of products to its retail client base – hence its strategic commitment to selling mutual funds and other investment products, life and non-life products via its brokerage subsidiary, as well as its core strength in mortgage origination and servicing. Corporate banking accounts for a modest 9% of total earnings, and Wells has no significant investment banking activity. In contrast, so-called community banking, essentially dealing with retail and small business clients via the branch network, accounts for 34% of the total.

Underpinning this product strategy is a strong sales culture, driven from the top of the bank, which is built around the metric of cross selling both in the retail and corporate bank. From only 3 products on average in 1989, the cross sell ratio has risen steadily to 5.7 in the retail sector by 2008 – a level superior to any of its US peers.

As indicated by Figure 8.7, the merged bank is now present in some 39 states with particular strength in the growth markets of Southern and Western US. The adjusted deposit-weighted annual projected population growth in its market area to 2013 is 7.6% against a peer average of 4.7%, and Wells has market-leading deposit shares in key growth markets such as Florida, Texas and Arizona.

Unlike so many of its US peers, Wells has eschewed expansion abroad and into investment banking despite repeated rumours – prior to the current crisis – that Wells might be a buyer of a major European bank. Its conservative stance has minimized damage from the current banking crisis despite Wells' position as a major US mortgage lender. In 2008, the bank established reserves against a portion of its home equity loans but avoided significant involvement with the sub-prime and structured products which brought down Wachovia.

In interviews several years ago with the author, Kovacevich outlined some of the basic principles of Wells' strategy:

> It's all about revenue. Banking is only growing at roughly the rate of GDP growth. Therefore you have to take market share. Why are we winning market share? Because we're passionate about selling. If you do anything for 20 years, you'll make it! Narrow-based companies are forced to take excess risk because, even when you know the macroeconomics will go against you, no one knows when, or has the guts to tell the stockholders 'I'm going to slow down the business' because you'll get killed by the competition. But a diversified financial service company has choices. You may not grow as fast as a pure play, but there's steady growth over time. I really believe that people will realize that we're in only one business – financial services, not banking.

> What does this mean for us? Some will decide to sell out, which will lead to a rapid consolidation of the industry. Financial services

are the only industry of size where the largest has only 3% of the market. It may take a long time, but it will happen.

Five years later, there has indeed been consolidation, but it would have been an imaginative observer to predict that Wells would be the principal beneficiary in the form that it took during the current crisis!

Strategy evaluation

Wells' consistent pursuit of a conservative product and client strategy over 20 years, culminating in a transforming acquisition at the depth of the major US banking crisis since the depression, is a role model of success for retail banks in other markets as well.

While the Wachovia acquisition poses obvious execution risks, the lessons of minimizing such risks going back to 1989 have been learned, and management believes that strong leadership, the principle of using 'best of breed' technology solutions, and minimizing customer disruption should minimize such risks. Continuity of management is another major contributor to its strategy; the current management team has worked together for decades.

Earnings growth in the next few years should be sustained by merger synergies and the application of Wells' selling culture to Wachovia's client base. Wells' stock has benefited from its superior performance during the banking crisis and should enable the company to continue to make acquisitions using its highly valued paper. Interestingly, Wells Fargo is the only core US bank holding of the highly regarded value investor Warren Buffett. While Wells lost its unique AAA rating among US banks as a result of the Wachovia exposure, our interviewees by and large agreed that it remains a role model for 'back to basics' banking – the ideal posited for the post-turmoil period.

To summarize several of the comments of our interviewees, Wells Fargo is a well-managed bank in a relatively slow growing market. And it does not engage in anything management cannot control.

9
Summary and Outlook

This final chapter is made up of three elements which pull together the findings of our research and conclude the book.

First is the author's synthesis of the interview findings. The sample of 25 interviews across the sector, including not only senior banking executives but also their consultants, banking analysts, rating agencies and regulators, cannot in any way be regarded as having any academic validity. It does, however, provide a useful contemporaneous insight early in 2009 of their frank opinions. It was widely acknowledged by our interviewees that the crisis still could evolve in new, unforeseen directions, and that key variables such as the future regulatory and ownership framework were far from resolved. In such cases, we try to indicate the possible directions.

Second is our summation of the lessons from our eight case studies of strategic success stories. Once again, further chapters in their evolution must be written for these institutions, and there is no guarantee that revisiting the issue in a year or so would produce the same or even similar listing. Yet they do reflect an expert, independent view of successful models at the time of writing which should be both durable as well as a possible model for other institutions.

Finally, we present our own view of the outlook for major bank strategies based on these inputs and our own experience from several decades of consulting and other research into the sector. We make a particular effort to identify issues which are unresolved at the time of writing and the direction best practice might take in addressing these issues.

1) Synthesis of the interview findings

We summarize briefly below our key findings from Chapters 3 through 7:

a) Generic lessons learned for the future from the banking crisis

– Excessive leverage and mistakes in real estate lending are, once again, the key drivers of this crisis as they have been for decades in the past.
– Successful risk management requires both extensive risk experience and judgement at the top of the bank, not delegated to technical specialists who lack this practical experience and may rely on faulty predictive models.
– Banks, regulators and rating agencies missed the forest for the trees. The systemic consequences of practices such as 'originate to distribute' and exclusive focus on the Tier 1 ratio were ignored. Regulatory practices generally focused solely on the individual bank and not on these systemic outcomes.
– There are serious limitations on the value of mathematical models, in particular when making assumptions in a time of systemic stress. Correlations in such periods cannot be relied upon for rating and other decisions.
– 'The enemy is us!' The growth model driven by a period of steady economic expansion involved all the constituencies concerned – not only the banks, but also investors, rating agencies, regulators and clients. Assigning blame for the outcome is thus not a particularly productive exercise.
– Regulatory and other practices in the downturn have been revealed as pro-cyclical. Thus the focus on Tier 1 led to higher systemic leverage, which has had to be addressed in a severe economic downturn in which liquidity and capital were in short supply.
– There are many flaws in the rating model: specifically the conflict of interest from having rated clients pay for ratings, and the use of correlation models used to create structured products. Whatever the outcome of the current debate on these issues, users in the future must rely more on their own analysis. The rating agencies no longer seem to benefit from their traditional advantage of better information.

b) Specific lessons for risk management

- The limitations of statistical models – in particular under stress conditions. 'Tail events' skew results in practice. Process has run ahead of human understanding.
- The lack of relevant risk experience at the top of major banks despite the complexity of current risk profiles. Top management in many banks has prioritized earnings growth rather than risk controls.
- A universal focus on the Tier 1 ratio, not a broader range of performance metrics such as liquidity and overall leverage. By 2007, liquidity had almost disappeared from the agenda of many banks and regulators because of the widespread assumption that the wholesale markets would provide it.
- The need to adjust performance measurement to the period of actual risk exposure. Bonuses were based on perceived current valuations which turned out to be erroneous. One result has been the current regulatory and official assault on bonuses and compensation – a classic case of locking the barn door after the horse had departed.
- Bank regulators made errors of commission (i.e., lack of focus on liquidity) and generally (with the exception of some like Bank of Spain with hands-on supervision) were not on top of actual practice. There was no victim during the good times!

c) How has the business model evolved as a result of the crisis?

Chapter 5 addressed a number of dimensions of the business model, which we summarize below:

1) Size and complexity issue

- There have been contrary factors at play. In the banking crisis, size and breadth are positives in providing support, but they also constrain entrepreneurship and creativity. More relevant is the issue of management quality: is there strong, disciplined and top-down management in such banks? Did they 'stick to their knitting' in businesses they knew or look outside for 'quick fixes' to provide earnings growth?
- Many so-called 'narrow' banking models failed or came close to failure in the crisis, in particular those dependent on market

funding. Thus monoline insurance, credit cards and consumer lending, and monoline mortgage providers fell apart as a result of asset quality problems and the drying up of the wholesale markets.

– Cross selling within a large, complex organization produced mis-allocation of resources, possible mis-selling and unhappy retail clients. Thus in an investment bank such as UBS priority was given to selling to retail clients, while the allocation of cheap retail funding to the trading desks led to the massive accumulation of toxic products.

– There has been a widespread call for simplicity and transparency in the business model with clear business line responsibility. Investors in particular have little faith in reported data, while the complexity of products and opacity of profit reporting have been an issue for all the relevant constituencies.

– The banking crisis itself has created yet more large, complex organizations, especially in the US banking system which had been relatively decentralized. For many observers, this is a move in the wrong direction: more complexity and opacity as well as concentration of economic power.

2) Future restructuring/M & A

– There is widespread agreement on the central role of government in the future in driving the restructuring of national banking systems. The political fallout from the billions of public funds spent recapitalizing banks has created another stakeholder whose views cannot be ignored in setting bank governance and strategy.

– One result of this infusion of public funds is the focus on national interests. In late 2008 and early 2009, most national authorities set out their strategic concerns, such as priority to domestic lending and national clients. A number of economic objectives, such as limits on bank compensation, were imposed, while more political and social objectives such as protecting the environment have been articulated as a trade-off for making available public funding.

– Major M & A transactions in banking to date have been largely shotgun marriages – essentially systemic consolidation to clear up the system. Many such deals, such as Wells/Wachovia and Lloyds/HBOS, are widely viewed as 'make or break' ones given the high perceived risks of taking over a problem business and the limitations of due diligence.

- It is widely agreed that there are currently few possible consolidators but many possible candidates. Several interviewees noted that transactions will take place among the second tier banks in response to concentration at the top of the sector, but the overall appetite for M & A risk is limited in the current environment.
- The stated investor desire for simplicity and transparency will lead to segment focus ('narrow down'), not a banking supermarket. Product innovation will take a back seat to focus on priority client needs. How durable these worthy objectives are, however, can only be tested over the long term!
- Such a 'back to basics' approach will lead to the sale or otherwise disposal of so-called 'non-core' businesses. This will be reinforced by the need to generate capital to pay back government investment. Priority in divestiture will be given to units which have not yet been fully integrated into the systems of the merged organization. Asset management units have been high on the list of possible disposals.

3) The regulatory impact

- While regulators have only begun to formulate their thinking, some trends are clear now. The relevant national political atmosphere/environment will play a major role. More regulation, more capital and more costly regulation will weigh especially on multi-national/global banks.
- The market is unlikely to see actual mergers of regulators – rather 'regulatory colleges' of those involved in a given bank's activities, which might be headed by a national authority. Our US regulators interviewed noted that even in the US, historical efforts to merge bank regulators have been unsuccessful.
- Consultants speak of a possible 'binary' strategic choice between a bank as a low-profit 'utility' and a more profitable 'narrow' bank – all depending on variables such as regulatory actions on capital. The concept of 'utilitization' – a bank in public ownership with its earnings regulated as a public utility – is of concern to a number of bankers in markets such as Europe.

- Regulators (and others!) would like to see less risk and complexity. Several interviewees argued for less innovation and more focus on the core banking business.

4) Product range

- There is a widespread view that banks should go 'back to basics', focusing on deposit gathering as well as customer loans and services, as opposed to fee income or putting capital at risk. Once again, one can argue how durable such strategies will be in a growth environment.
- The repricing of such deposits and loans should make them much more profitable. Remuneration for these core products prior to the banking crisis had collapsed to uneconomic levels. In addition, savings rates from a macro-economic standpoint should rise in markets like the US and the UK, enhancing their growth potential. Banks should 'go for the cash'!
- Wealth management, cash management, securities services and similar cash-related businesses will be given priority in an effort to reduce reliance on the wholesale markets. While wealth management is attractive, if only as a vehicle to retain client deposits, it was noted that few banks have the scale to be successful in the business.
- Most observers believe investment banking will not only shrink as a business but also become much less profitable as the 'shadow banking system' becomes less important. Those interviewees who ventured estimates of investment banking profitability generally placed the business at the lower end of ROE attractiveness.
- Among the possible 'non-core' businesses to be divested, asset management is a prime candidate. In markets like France and Spain, this trend has been accentuated by the current market downturn.

5) Clients

- There is agreement that commercial banks should focus on segments like high net worth individuals and SME who generate significant volumes of cash.

- Given the dismal current outlook for capital raising and trading in the traditional capital markets, investment banks should focus on distressed debt and corporate re-financing.

6) Geography

- Our interviewees agree that emerging markets in general remain relatively attractive because of a continued macro-economic growth differential, but more differentiation within that segment will allow for political and economic problems. Not all BRICs are equal! The macro-economic and political problems in the Central and Eastern Europe (CEE) and Russia have cooled bankers' strategic interest in such markets.
- There is likely to be a re-focus on the home market for political as well as economic reasons. Authorities such as the Swiss have explicitly taken such regulatory action, while others in Europe have also made clear their political preference for domestic lending.
- A key issue for banks going forward is the desired balance or trade-off between geographic diversity and focus. For many interviewees, market 'footprint' or share is important in foreign markets both for economies of scale and market penetration. Thus a bank like Santander will argue for a focused penetration of a limited number of national markets, while HSBC will emphasize its global presence.

7) Investor model

- To judge from our survey, there has been a total transformation from the old model of investor objectives (high ROE, high earnings growth) to de-leveraging, de-risking and greater simplicity or transparency. Yet we found no investor who would deny the long-term attractions of earnings growth!
- At present, bank stock investors are confused and fearful, with little trust in bank financial numbers or management statements. The result is that bank stocks generally sell well below book value as opposed to a multiple of it before the crisis.

8) Overall conclusions

- There is no ideal business model for the future, and many key variables which might drive this model are unknown at present.

Investors are watching carefully the outcome of the current economic crisis – in particular the success of some of the major bailouts and government policy as stockholders.
- As discussed below, other factors such as management quality must be factored into the equation. Clearly, the presence of superior management quality can overcome relative weakness in the business model.
- Finally, as analysed later in this chapter, preferences on business model have been known to change over time!

2) Conclusions from our case studies

As mentioned above, our eight case studies were selected largely on the basis of recommendations by our interviewees. In most cases, we were able to supplement the case studies with direct interviews with senior management of the bank involved, but we also accessed rating agency and analyst reports. The focus in our selection was the actual business model chosen, recognizing that individual banks might suffer setbacks which might not, however, invalidate that particular business model. The ability to navigate the current banking crisis was clearly one of the key variables driving this selection.

Recognizing the limitations of this selection process, we feel that the following observations can be drawn from our analysis of the case studies.

- *None have appeared to want to revise or dramatically change the chosen model.* The core choice of products, client segments and geographic markets seems to remain in place. Perhaps the most interesting case study in this respect is Goldman Sachs, who steadfastly maintains that its business strategy will not change despite the bank's shift in regulation to that of a commercial bank under the Federal Reserve system – as well as the dramatic transformation in its business environment. While that view might change with a possible acquisition or other development, it is a vote of confidence in a model which has, albeit with some damage, survived the banking crisis to date.

  The same applies to the other banks in our sample. HSBC will remain a global bank focusing on the strategic linkages among its wide variety of businesses, while JPMorgan Chase will retain its six core business units. Santander has resisted criticism of its opportunistic approach to acquisitions while retaining its core retail and geographic focus. Wells Fargo now has a national retail franchise but the same business focus on the retail/SME sectors. Banco Itau is consummating a major merger but retaining its core domestic strategy. Standard Chartered remains committed to its emerging market focus.

And UBS continues to sustain its triple presence in asset management, investment banking and global wealth management, all supported by a major domestic banking presence in its home market. In our case study we have suggested that the wealth management business could exist without the other two major components, and there are perennial rumours about divestiture and restructuring of the other businesses. But the fact remains that, for the time being, the in-depth strategic review undertaken by the new management team in 2007–2009 has not yet produced any major strategic transformation.

- *While several of the sample banks have suffered from the banking crisis, to date their realized losses have not seriously impaired their earning power.* By and large, they have 'stuck to their knitting', although that knitting might have been unprofitable for an earnings quarter or two, as was the case for Goldman which reported its first quarterly loss since going public. Most have continued to report profits for the year 2008 despite such a hit. Santander, Banco Itau and Standard Chartered actually reported increased earnings in what was the worst year in decades on record for most banks. Earnings were down compared to 2007 for HSBC and JPMorgan, but the former's principal problem has been sub-prime losses on loans made well before the crisis. And UBS' wealth management business continued to perform well despite some loss of clients and lower margins.

Whether these relatively favourable results will continue as the crisis unfolds is a major unknown, but the results to date are impressive in a market overwhelmed by bad news.

- *A common feature of the case study banks is their disciplined, top-down, risk-oriented management.* In many cases the CEO or chairman – and the culture he imparts – has been in place for an extended period of time. Yet at the same time this discipline is consistent with an occasional opportunity initiative. Emilio Botin is perhaps the role model for such 'disciplined opportunism' – as demonstrated by his lucrative exit from the ABN AMRO takeover disaster. In the US, Dick Kovacevich turned his scorn for big mergers on a dime when he bid successfully for Wachovia. And Itau's transforming merger with Unibanco is a similar example of seizing a transforming opportunity.

Tight top-down risk management has been a byword for Jamie Dimon at JPMorgan. But banks like Wells Fargo, HSBC and Goldman are also role models for such a culture. Risk-taking has been refined to an art at Goldman, which has survived losses several times in its history which might have destroyed another institution. The issue for us is whether the risks are understood by management, which was not the case in many institutions who failed during the crisis. A salutary lesson is the negative impact on HSBC's earnings in recent years from their entry into the US subprime market, which has had a much greater negative impact on its subsequent earnings than any other factor.

The relevant phrase for such successful CEOs is 'disciplined'. As indicated in our interviews, observers have had their fill of charismatic leaders who promised continued earnings growth but did not address the risks involved.

- *In all this analysis, we should acknowledge the success of thousands of smaller retail banks – community banks in the US, building societies in the UK, savings and cooperative banks across the world – who have not only survived but also thrived during the crisis.* In this book they collectively are Sherlock Holmes' classic 'dog that didn't bark'! Such institutions are the role models for the 'back to basics' strategy recommended by so many of our interviewees.

- *Our case studies confirm that there is no one single desirable banking strategy.* In effect, there are 'many roads to Rome'. The critical factor, as consultants never tire of pointing out, is the ability to achieve relative competitive advantage. When asked to cite possible ranges of ROE for the future, many of our interviewees suggested a spread of results driven largely by such competitive advantage. For Goldman, it may be the ability to manage risk profitably. For HSBC or UBS Wealth Management, it may be the global brand. For Wells Fargo and Santander, it may be running an efficient and customer-oriented retail network. In contrast, many of the 'narrow' banks who have disappeared in the crisis had only one advantage: a low-cost, standard product sustained by inexpensive wholesale funding which melted away in the turmoil.

- *The voice of the investor was clear from our interviews in what he did NOT want, but there was much less clarity on the key issue of growth.* This critical dimension is what created the old model which ultimately drove the banking crisis. And yet all of our case study institutions continue their commitment to strategies of sustained growth. What will be the result? Clearly, most of these banks are anticipating slower growth as banking earnings cease growing or actually shrink in relation to GDP expansion, but where might the balance lie? The fear of 'utilitization' in some countries reflects fears that banks may be repressed if they are seen to be driving for unacceptable growth. We express our own views on this critical issue below!

3) Our own views for the future

At this final stage of our research, we move beyond the results of our interview sample and case study analysis and offer our personal appraisal of the way forward for major banks.

- *Uncertainty!* At this stage (early 2009) of our research, it has been suggested that it is foolhardy to make any prognostications which can be shattered by subsequent events – as they have been so often since mid-2007! If we have a rationale for doing so, it is that the banking sector crossed the uncertainty 'Rubicon' in late 2008 when the US and other Western governments, in effect, committed the necessary taxpayer funds to rescue their banking systems. The structure of these systems, their profitability and other variables are yet to be shaped by the impact of the subsequent economic downturn, but at least that particular uncertainty has largely disappeared.
- *There will be a recovery!* None of our sources argued that we have embarked on an infinite downward slope to disaster! Whether recovery commences in 2010, as in the standard forecast, or later, is open to argument, but none of our sample banks is planning on a Japanese-style outcome in which banks are effectively marginalized as economic factors with returns at or below the

cost of capital. Thus growth is a long-term assumption, and bank strategies are still keyed to that assumption.

- *The outcome will be a dynamic one.* The standard forecast from our interviewees calls for a massive shift in strategy to deposit generation and repricing of the traditional loan and deposit products. Yet history suggests that the most likely longer term outcome is a more dynamic and complex one. Market forces will once again drive down the profitability of this 'back to basics' behaviour. For most large banks, to rely purely on a 'back to basics' traditional retail strategy would be naïve. Smaller retail banks close to their customer base have succeeded in earning satisfactory returns, but for the major banking institutions this is not an equilibrium position. For example, wholesale funding is under a cloud today, but it is difficult to envisage how a dynamic banking system can survive without some capital market activity supplementing customer deposits.

  In short, we believe growth will return as a major driver of bank strategy as well as bank stock valuations. The heady valuations of 2–3 times book value may not return, but there will be differentiation in bank valuations with a premium paid for perceived growth potential.

- *We'll be here again!* Perhaps the most distressing – but also credible – comment of so many of our interviewees is that the current crisis, however damaging it has been, will not be the last! Each crisis is 'different', but in a capitalist environment there is a certain sameness to the series of crises in the Western world since the 1930s. This leads to the question which follows!

- *Can regulators, governments and rating agencies master the market forces which drive this volatility?* The evidence from our interviews is not particularly positive. As some interviewees have pointed out, in a similar future boom there may be no obvious 'victims' and therefore apparent need for intervention. The enemy is indeed 'all of us!' As various chairmen of the US Federal Reserve Board have found, metaphorically taking the drinks away from a raging cocktail party is not very popular. Whistle blowers are rarely welcome! Opinions on the relative quality of the professionals in these agencies differ, but history is not on the side of the optimists.

  There will certainly be a raft of new regulatory controls on leverage, liquidity and other risks after this crisis. A future 'Basel III'

will impose such through-the-cycle standards, and the pro-active
stance of regulators such as the Bank of Spain should become more
widespread. But at the end of the day, individual regulators and
rating agencies have to have the courage to act as the boom swells,
and the track record is not brilliant.

- *Investors do 'move from one side of the boat to the other' in their so-
  called 'models'.* As Simon Samuels points out in his analogy above,
  investors in bank stocks today – as well as governments who have
  funded bailouts – are shell shocked from the barrage of bad news
  and uncertainties. Their instinctive reaction is thus to de-risk the
  business in every respect. A more potent factor may be the much
  feared 'utilitization' of bank securities, whether actually national-
  ized or not. How likely is the return to an earlier era when bank
  stocks were perceived as solid providers of a dividend yield? We
  don't know, but certainly the political climate in some European
  countries may lead in this direction.

  How transparent and predictable can bank earnings be in the
  future? Certainly, the advent of complex derivative-based products
  and off-balance sheet obligations brought reporting complexity to
  a new level in 2007–2009. Yet with all the wisdom of rating agencies and modern accounting methods, many banking institutions
  will remain opaque in the eyes of the investor. This opacity will
  have to be addressed in valuation parameters.

- *Revenge of the SMEs!* Along with retail clients as a source of deposit
  funds, we found in our interview series a widespread apprecia-
  tion of the value of small- and mid-sized businesses (SMEs) across
  the banking universe. Once the poor relation falling between the
  larger stools of retail and corporate banking, the SME segment has
  been increasingly recognized by bank management as a priority
  target for virtually all of its key products: reliable deposits, profitable loans and wealth management for its owners as well as other
  products to be cross sold.

- *The future of rating agencies*: Despite the trenchant and widespread
  criticism of a 'broken business model' articulated in our interviews, it is difficult to suggest an alternative. Having apparently
  lost their unique value added as a semi-insider, agencies are still
  needed as an independent source of valuation. They will presumably address the challenges made to their valuation models.
  Whether they can adjust their business model – to eliminate the

obvious conflict of interest in being paid by the banks they rate – is another question. In the future, however, their ratings will be subject to a market test as credit default swaps (CDS) become increasingly efficient and relevant as a market price.

- *Return to sustainable growth as a bank strategy!* What conclusions can be drawn from our research on the title of this book – strategies for sustained growth? The evidence from our case studies is that each one continues to pursue such a growth strategy. For Goldman Sachs, it is an opportunistic, market-driven one based on a balancing of risk and reward. For Santander, Itau, JPMorgan Chase and Wells Fargo, in the short term it involves extracting the benefits from recent major acquisitions. For HSBC and UBS Wealth Management, it is to continue to leverage their worldwide brand and physical network, while Standard Chartered will continue to invest in its growth geographies.

A major challenge in the longer term for some is the limitation of the home market. Thus Itau and Wells Fargo at some point may have to invest in product or physical expansion outside home base. Yet Santander and JPMorgan Chase have already built such product or geographic diversity into their business model.

As the much quoted aphorism (attributed to the American baseball player Yogi Berra) states, 'predicting is always a problem, especially about the future!' Yet in today's turbulent banking world, such profitable and healthy banks are among the few who are in a position to pick and choose their growth options.

Bibliography

Boston Consulting Group, *Point of View, Outlook and Evergreens*, presentation by Andy Maguire to International Bank Planners Forum, 7 November 2008, London.

Citigroup Global Markets, *What If: Applying Previous Crises to Today's European Bank Sector*, 2008, London.

Citigroup Global Markets, *Over the Hill: What Will 'normal' Bank Profitability Look Like?* 5 September 2008, London.

Citigroup Global Markets, *A Crisis of Confidence: Reflections on the Credit Crisis*, presentation by Simon Samuels to the International Bank Planners Forum, 9 May 2008, London.

Davis, Steven I., *Leadership in Financial Services: Lessons For the Future*, Macmillan, London, 1997.

Davis, Steven I., *Excellence in Banking – Revisited!* Palgrave Macmillan, London, 2004.

Economist, *Confessions of a Risk Manager: A Personal View of the Crisis*, 9 August 2008, London.

McKinsey & Co, *Après le Deluge*, presentation by Hugh Harper to International Bank Planners Forum, November 2007.

Merrill Lynch, *2009 Year Ahead: Remaining Cautious*, 19 December 2008, London.

Index